SINGER'S CAREER GUIDE TO THE ENTERTAINMENT INDUSTRY

BY

PEGGY M. CROCKER

ISBN: 1-4033-3986-4 (e-book)
ISBN: 1-4033-3987-2 (Paperback)
ISBN: 1-4033-3988-0 (Hardcover)

This book is printed on acid free paper.

1stBooks – rev. 04/03/03

The Basic Steps to Superstardom

How to tell if you have talent...Developing your voice...Singing with a band...Performing for pay...Moving up and branching out...Stage presence...knowing your audience...Getting ready for one of the Music Cities and how to network when you arrive...Where to find information and how to use it...Where and how to enter national competitions...touring in and out of the US...When and how to work with the music business professionals...How to deal with the media...Songwriting and the singer...and much more.

Realistic what-to-do and how-to-do-it guidelines from beginning your career to getting your foot in the door of the top people in this business called music.

Although this book was written for the beginning singer, it could benefit musicians, small and medium market promoters, agents and managers, and business teachers of the art, as well.

FOR THERESA

A SPECIAL DEDICATION

In loving memory of Virginia Connor, the sweet and beautiful granddaughter of the late, great singing legend Patsy Cline and Charlie Dick. Virginia was killed instantly at the age of 15 in an automobile accident, while on her way home from a Christmas church function on December 17, 1994.

Members of her family, friends, the Pasty Cline Scholarship Foundation, the Pasty Cline Fan Club, and everyone who knew Virginia, will forever miss her.

ACKNOWLEDGMENTS

Special thanks to Pete and Mary Jean Hall who afforded me many opportunities I might not otherwise have had by accepting me into their family and opening their hearts and home on my many trips to Nashville. And thanks to Alice Detrick for being the wonderful singer she is and for introducing me to good friends like the Halls and Joan and Lee Salmen, who drove us to Nashville in their beautiful motor coach.

There are many other people who deserve recognition, for without them this book may not have been written: Linwood Crandall (An English teacher who inspired the writer in me.), Wayne Hurst (my best friend), the Cormier family, Jack Cox and the Silver Dollar band, Earl and Mary Ruth Dixon (and daughter Sherrie), Dee Wayne White (father of award-winning music arranger—Bergen White) for the many music courses in college, Sylvia Wilt (sister of Patsy Cline), Hilda Hensley (mother of Patsy Cline), Hal Herman (music theatre director at Shenandoah University), Linde Herman, Wayne and Judy Dalton, Charles and Lola Madagan, Louis and Ellen Ruffner, Barbara Bouchard, Margaret MacLaughlin, Roy and Diane Dixion, Joe Faires (East Coast Promoter), Tracee and Jim Wink, Dottie O'Dailey, John Dube', Sylvia Shirey, Melvin J. Dick (brother to Charlie), Eddie Munden, James D.Thompson, Barry Lee Bowser, Leah Streetman, Christopher Owens (Artistic director of the Wayside Theatre), Tamara Johnson, Dave Ryan, Dona Gilliam, (music department at James Madison University), Dale Leatherman (author of "Courting Danger"), Bob Naylor, Donnelle Oxley, Jeremy Owens, Country Plus's Sherry and Dave Schroeder, and my Nashville friends: Charlie Dick (husband of the late Patsy Cline), Dave and Charlotte Thornhill, Bob Bean, Zoe Tapscott, Michael Twitty (son of the late Conway), Kimberly Jo Herron, Dick and Goldie Herron, Vickie, Tory, and Wayne Bailey, Paul Busdiecker, and Mason Hall.

And thank's to every major artist I ever interviewed or worked with.

Thank you to Theresa Cormier for teaching me what to expect from young aspiring singers—what a talent!

CONTENTS

INTRODUCTION

SINGER'S CAREER GUIDE TO THE ENTERTAINMENT INDUSTRY—

the basics of starting and following through with a singing Career—was written because of the many times someone asked me a simple question: "I am talented and I want to sing. How do I go about getting started?"

In order to properly answer that question I concluded it was necessary to write a book that would guide the beginner from singing the first note to developing a career in the competitive world of singing.

The definition of a career is "a profession for which one trains—a course of continued progress—which is undertaken for the purpose of achieving a permanent place in that chosen profession."

A course of continued process. Think about what that means: a step-by-step process in which you thoroughly master the first step before moving on to the next—a positive and practical approach.

Using this approach, you become absorbed in the learning process, but you stay in control. This takes a lot of dedication and determination. If you let the learning process become one of frustration and negativity, it consumes you and you lose the control, and thus your ability to reach your goals.

When you are starting out—and throughout your career—you will run into people who will tell you that it's a backstabbing, cut-throat business, that not very many people make it, that the competition is too tough, and that it's a lot more difficult today than it used to be. As I see it, it's not necessarily more difficult than it used to be, it's just different.

The music artists of the past had to work hard and long, travelling in cars, buses, and any other way they could to make their performances. Sometimes they had to leave their families for months on end for very little financial reward, especially the country artists.

Gone are the days when an artist can just "pop" into a music manager's office, pull out the guitar, and give an instant audition.

Gone are the days when an artist or manager can "drop by" the radio station and get instant air play.

But you are living in a time of high technology and better communication. Now artists have more choices in venues, diversity of performance, and are involved in the decision-making process in every aspect of their careers.

Today's music artist still works very hard and puts in long hours, but once an artist has achieved some level of success he or she travels in comfortable style, stays in beautiful accommodations, and is often able to bring his family along on tour. The competition may be tougher because the artist has to be better prepared, but the financial rewards are also greater. You should view today's competition as an exciting, challenging opportunity, because that is what it is.

With Los Angeles and Nashville working on projects together, and Las Vegas and Branson, MO. sharing performers, the opportunities are endless. Country music has exploded, crossing into all areas of the entertainment industry. It is, as Barbara Mandrell once sang about, definitely "cool to be country."

Since most of my music business experience has been in the country music field, I refer often to that particular genre; however, the same basic principles apply to all aspiring singers.

Music is the Universal Language of Mankind.
-Longfellow

PART I

GETTING STARTED

In moving toward a career in music, it is important to know what you want to achieve and what you are willing to sacrifice in order to achieve it. It is necessary to have attainable goals in order to be clearly focused for each step in the process. No one can guarantee the successes of another individual. Your destiny is up to you. The "Singer's Career Guide" will show you the path many successful singers have taken before you. If you list your goals, read this book (starting at the very beginning), and if you are sincerely dedicated to becoming a successful singer, you will have what it takes to climb to the top.

CHAPTER 1

♪

TALENT AND ABILITIES

BEGINNING THE CLIMB

"I am talented and I want to sing. How do I get started?"

The first step to a singing career, at any level, is to have the ability, the talent to do it. The second step is to have the right attitude, to be a team player. And the third step is to have stamina, the tenacity to stick to it. Talent, tenacity and teamwork, the three Ts of career management.

Ask yourself these three questions: Can I really carry a tune? Can I truly be open-minded with others? Can I accept criticism? If you answered "yes" to all of these questions, then you possess the ability to start developing your talent.

DEVELOPING YOUR TALENT

It is essential to have good pitch and a good ear for music. You must be able to sing on key and to lead musicians in song. How can you test your pitch by yourself? One exercise that you can do is to sing on a tape recorder and play it back to listen for clarity and pitch; later on, listen for believability. (This will be discussed later.) If you are not sure about your own listening abilities, ask someone you trust to listen to your tape. People close to you sometimes have the tendency not to want to hurt your feelings, but if you are off key, you need to know.

A great way to work out little problems is to sing along with tapes of melody only and play them back until you feel comfortable with them. There are companies that specialize in cassette reproductions without lyrics. One such company is called Sound Choice, 14100 South Lakes Drive, Charlotte, NC 28273. Sound Choice acquires the rights to produce radio play versions of all types of music for marketing purposes. They reproduce 4 songs onto a CDG+, video, or cassette. One side of a cassette (for example) will be a full production demo tape of the vocal likeness of a major recording artist while the other side maintains the full production, minus the lead vocals. Sound Choice also is a Karaoke dealer, with sing-a-long machines small enough for home use and large enough for nightclubs. Although Sound Choice can be reached directly at (800) 326-1894, they suggest going through your local music store which might save you shipping and handling costs or any discounts being offered.

For other Karaoke Dealers check the local electronic stores or the telephone directories. Most public and college libraries have directories for all the major cities in the United States. These sing-along-machines can be fun, but may be a little too expensive at this stage of your career (ranging from $200 to $1000 and up). If this is the case, then drop a cassette in your own boom box or tape recorder and sing away.

VOCAL COACH

If you cannot correct minor vocal problems yourself, then it's strongly recommended that you hire a vocal coach before going ahead with your career.

A good place to start looking for a vocal coach is at a high school, college, or church. Ask the music director if he does private tutoring in vocals or if he would recommend an advanced student of music. If there are not any schools in your community which offer this service, look in the yellow pages of the telephone book or the local newspaper classified ads under "Instruction," or check with a piano teacher; he usually can help with your vocal exercises and breathing techniques.

When I decided that I wanted to sing, I had no idea where to find a good vocal coach. I was listening to late-night television and heard a singer mention her coach, Todd Duncan, the original Porgy in "Porgy and Bess" and director of the choir and music productions at the Catholic University in Washington, D.C. I immediately knew I had to audition for him. Luckily, I was able to obtain his telephone number through Information and called to schedule an appointment. He could tell I was a beginner, but he graciously granted me an audition. Now what was I to do? I didn't even have a song to sing.

I contacted a student from the Peabody Conservatory in Baltimore, Maryland, and he agreed to help me learn a song. Because

I liked the way Montserrat Caballe' sang "O Mio Babbino Caro," one of Puccini's arias, that's what I decided to learn. It didn't matter that I didn't speak a word of Italian and had never sung opera; I liked that song.

At the audition Mr. Duncan accepted me graciously into his home and his studio. He even kept his piano accompanist at the studio just for me. I was impressed. I was singing my little heart out when I fully realized what I was doing—singing for Todd Duncan. My knees began to wobble and I stopped. Mr. Duncan started where I left off, and a few notes later I picked it back up and began singing again. When I completed the aria, this kind man gave me his critique. "I can certainly understand why you want to sing; you have a nice voice range. But your Italian is lousy." Now there was an honest appraisal.

Then he explained that his schedule was filled with professional singers, but he said, "I want you to call a student of mine and tell him that I want him to give you lessons." I did, he did—until a year later when he moved to New York. The point is, I found a vocal coach. Today I would be better prepared, but I didn't have this book to guide me.

BREATHING TECHNIQUES

The vocal coach will help you with proper breathing exercises, as well as technical vocal exercises that will allow you to develop to your full potential. It is important to understand how breathing properly relates to being a good singer. Proper breathing techniques will eventually become second nature, and you will notice how easily the voice flows with clarity of word. There is a muscle in the center of your body called the diaphragm (more on this later). It helps to control the lungs and movement of air. Singing from the diaphragm (the abdominal area), rather than the throat, gives the voice a clear focused sound and aids in achieving good pitch. When used correctly, your body will help you in developing your singing voice.

Once you have the ability to sing—the talent—the next step is being a team player.

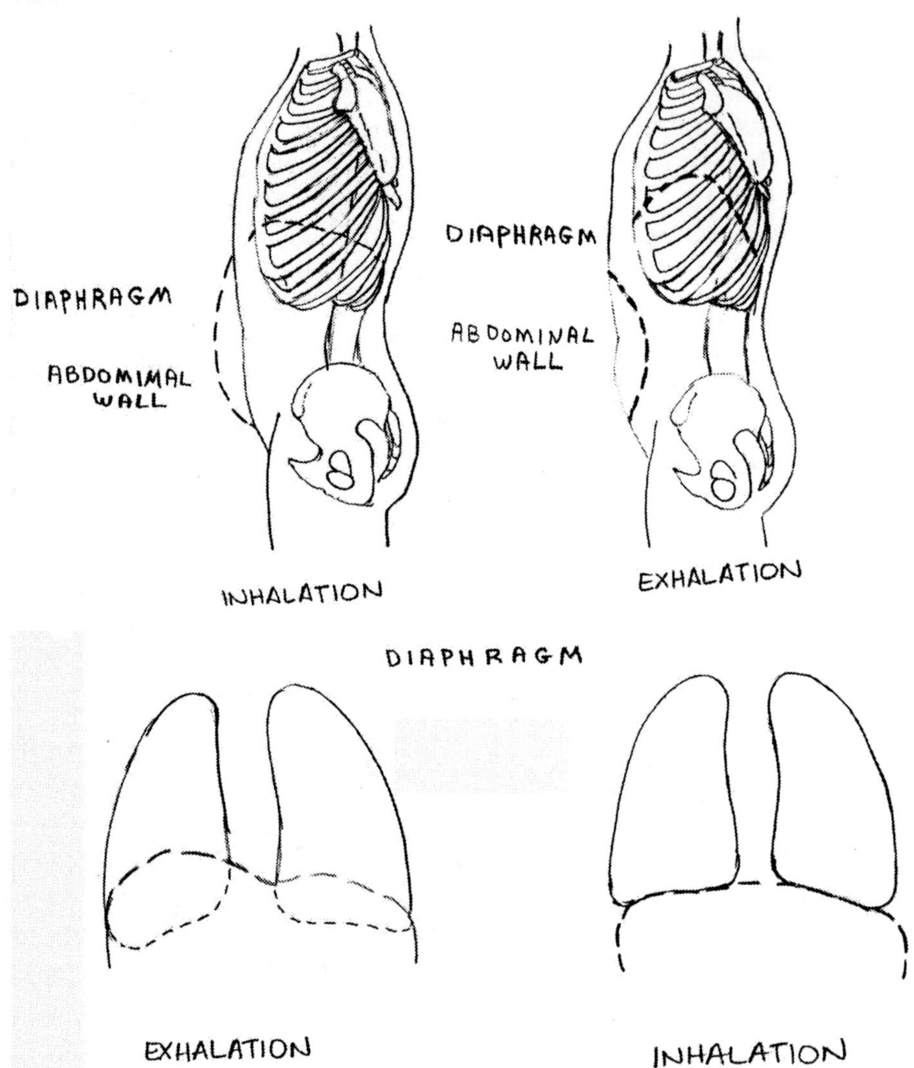
DIAPHRAGM
ABDOMIMAL WALL
DIAPHRAGM
ABDOMINAL WALL
INHALATION
EXHALATION
DIAPHRAGM
EXHALATION
INHALATION

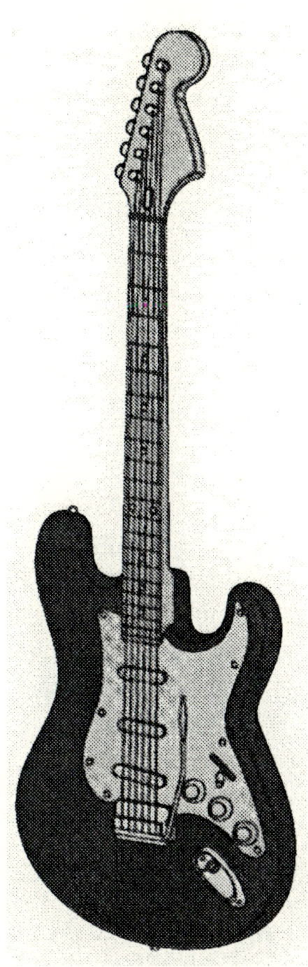

CHAPTER 2

♪

SINGING WITH A BAND

There are two ways to go about singing with a band; join an existing band or form your own. Which one should you do and how do you go about doing it?

First, stay in your own area. You probably aren't ready to leave home and travel with a band. Moving can be difficult on the finances and on you. You will have more confidence closer to family and friends. So unless you have plenty of money, several good contacts, and a lot of experience, stay close to home until you are ready. (When to branch out will be discussed later.)

JOIN AN EXISTING BAND

It would be an ideal situation if you joined an existing band for several logical reasons: money, reputation, and experience. It is important to join a band that is musically tight. A bad band can ruin your reputation fast. A good band already has an established reputation and is one that works every weekend and all holidays; this means you can start making money immediately.

How do you find an existing band that needs a lead singer? Advertise in the local paper and in the local music publication. Watch these same sources for bands that are looking for a lead singer. Place a request on the college and local community center bulletin boards, check with your local night club owners, or tell the personnel at the local music store, record shops, and electronic stores. And tell all of your musical friends. When you land an audition, it is important to feel comfortable with the other members and to check out their musical abilities, as well as your own. If there just aren't any opportunities to join a band, and you simply can't wait, then consider forming your own.

When I decided to join a band, I'd heard about a musician who owned a local service station. I introduced myself to him and asked if I could come to one of his rehearsal sessions. That was my introduction to the country music field. I found country music was fun; it was about life and living, the stuff our lives are made of. The guys humored me and let me sing a few songs at their local performances. It was only later that I realized I preferred managing a band, not singing in one.

FORM YOUR OWN BAND

Forming your own band is not an easy task, but is done all the time. First, you must use every means to get the word out, including advertising in the want ads.

The most important element of finding the right band members (other than talent) is attitude. Are they team players? I can not stress this enough. The band and lead singer are a team; there are no stars at this point. All band members should own and be responsible for their instrument, amplifier, and any needed effects units. As the lead singer, you should own your own microphone and have a prepared song list. The microphone is part of your sound system or public address system. The song list should include the keys in which you sing.

MUSICIANS

You will need to interview a drummer, lead guitar player, keyboard, rhythm guitar player, and a bass drum guitar player. If you are not sure how to go about this, find someone you trust who has this expertise.

When interviewing band members, ask them the following questions:

* What type of music do they play and listen to?
* How often are they willing to rehearse?
* How often do they want to play in public?
* What are their goals?

What about conflicts in their lives—family, school schedules, other activities or organizations they belong to, and relationships that could interfere with their rehearsal time or availability for performances. Find out early on if a spouse or boy/girl friend would have a problem with a lead singer of the opposite sex.

It is also important to find out about personal habits such as being on time, use of drugs or alcohol, and personal hygiene. Some band members drink alcohol on stage. In some states, the Alcohol Control Board does not permit this.

Each band should have a good sound system. The PA system consists of the lead and back-up singer's microphones, two speakers, connecting cables, and a mixing board. (See diagram in this chapter.) Go to a reputable local music store, talk to other band leaders about whom you've heard good reports, check with a sound company (Use the yellow pages), and ask a local club owner if you could look at another local band's PA sheet. The PA system should be included with each band's promotional package.

Club owners and promoters get promo-packages before booking the band. Tell the club owner/manager that you are forming a band and could use his or her help. Most people enjoy helping a sincere beginner. See the PA system listed in this chapter for a basic sound system that will get you started and will do a good job.

Some establishments do not have good stage lighting, so the band should consider getting a set of lights. Check with the same people you talk to about the sound equipment regarding type and costs of lighting, In the beginning, lighting might be a luxury item and most clubs have some type of lighting already. But if you run into a club that doesn't, perhaps you could borrow or rent lights for that one performance. Later on, you definitely will want your own.

REHEARSALS

Your PA system and lights have either been rented or purchased, the song list is in place, and the band has been formed. The next step is to make a cassette tape of all the songs on your list and give each band member a copy. Using a home recorder will work fine for this.

Each band member should practice at home to sharpen their own skills, so that rehearsals are used for tightening the group. The most important thing a band can do is make a commitment to rehearse regularly—and then keep that commitment. Remember, you are forming a business; it is vital to keep personal matters and gossip out of rehearsals. Do however, set aside a non-rehearsal time for non-musical issues or gripes.

During rehearsals, stick to the job, and you will reach your goals a lot more quickly. Two or three solid nights of stringent rehearsing is far better than meeting every night and wasting some of the rehearsal time. You've heard that practice makes perfect. It also gets you pay for performance.

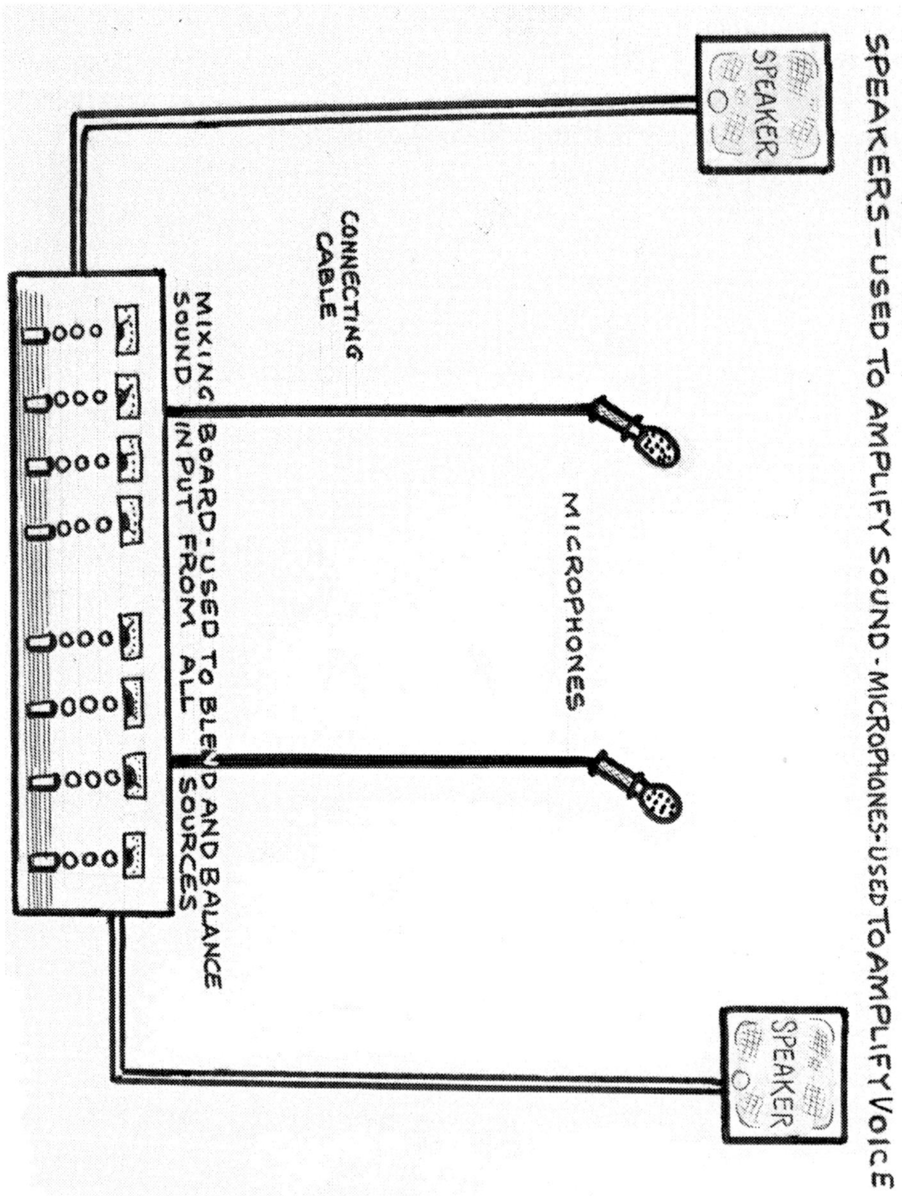
SPEAKERS—USED TO AMPLIFY SOUND-MICROPHONES-USED TO AMPLIFY VOICE
SPEAKER
SPEAKER
CONNECTING CABLE
MICROPHONES
MIXING BOARD-USED TO BLEND AND BALANCE
SOUND IN PUT FROM ALL SOURCES

BASIC PA SYSTEM

POWER MIXER (Mixing Board—blends and balances sound)

* A PV power mixer is reliable and can take a lot of abuse. Estimated cost: $700.00.
* You should use no less than an 8-channel power mixer, but if you decide to mike the drums you'll need a 12-channel.

If the salesperson asks you if you are in the market for a PA, tell him you are only looking for a power mixer.

SPEAKERS (used to amplify sound)

- Two PVS-P2 are all that's necessary, and will cost about $800 for both. Keep it simple.

MICROPHONE (used to amplify the voice)

- Shure model SM58 (lead, plus any background—back-up). This should cost about $150.00.

CABLES (connect speakers to power mixer)

- With the PV powered mixer, you will need a cable to each speaker. Estimated cost: $30.00 for two.

The two largest cable manufactures are Rapco Company and Horizons.

This is a suggestion for a very basic system. There are other reputable brand names and manufacturers. Music stores and club owners can tell you what systems other bands are using. Prices may vary depending on availability and supply and demand.

CHAPTER 3

PERFORMING FOR PAYMENT

BENEFIT SHOWS

To gain initial experience and recognition, you and your band may want to consider playing for local events at no charge. You are new to the music circuit, need experience, and need something to list on your resume. With free performances, you get the recognition you need and the organization benefits as well.

To go about this, read bulletins boards at music stores, record shops, local restaurants and clubs. Talk to your local radio stations. Read the entertainment section of the newspaper. Contact the person in charge and offer to perform at his next event for the publicity.

Do this as often as you need to, until you feel confident enough to work for pay. The audience's reaction will let you know when that time comes.

Getting paid for a performance means that you are ready to accept serious responsibilities.

CLUBS

In a night club, the true measure of a professional is starting on time, keeping the music moving and the customers dancing, taking only short breaks, and not quitting until the scheduled time. The key is whether the customers are having fun. That is number one. If the customers are happy, they will tell their friends, the club fills up, and the club owner/manager is happy.

When you've made owner/managers happy, you'll be asked back often. Word will get around and other clubs will become interested in you. If you create excitement for those party animals, you'll have all the work you can handle. Create hype.

During your performance, make announcements about the club's upcoming events. Ask the owner/manager if he or she would mind if you placed your mailing list cards on every table. The card should state the band's name and telephone number, and should ask for names and addresses of people who would like to be on the band's mailing list. Some bands put flyers on the tables announcing where they will be performing next, although some club owners/managers prohibit this practice. Remember, you are a business, and in business it is never a good idea to promote one establishment while being paid by another. The exception may be when you have a big event coming up in a venue that is not in direct competition with the club you're working for.

Sending schedule sheets with mailing list forms attached, are a good way to accumulate followers. People who have filled out your cards will more than likely give the additional form to a friend, and because people rarely go to clubs alone, they will bring this friend to your performances; later, that friend will bring another friend.

When fans receive their personal copy of your schedule, they will probably feel a connection to your group. It is important to know who your fans are.

So create hype with good planning. And remember that word of mouth is the best form of promotion.

CONTRACTS

When you perform for pay you should have a signed contract. A simple contract is sufficient at clubs, lounges, lodges, or any small venue. It should state the who, where, when, what, and why, plus any special requirements. The contract should be signed by you and the person responsible for contracting with the entertainers. There is a sample of a simple booking contract included in this chapter.

You may want to create your own contract, one that suits your particular style. It will be a legally binding contract without an attorney. The contract ensures the establishment that you will show up to perform, and it ensures that you will get paid a specific amount on a specific date for a specific performance. Contractual agreements should not be left to memory—or to blind trust.

Sometimes clubs double-book. Perhaps the person was very busy and forgot to write the booking down, and perhaps he forgot that another contract was previously signed with a different band. This doesn't happen very often, but when it does, it is usually an honest mistake. Unless it happens more than once at the same club, or you were the first booking, let the club off the hook. Take the night off, and because you were such a nice person, suggest two bookings next month.

BASIC BOOKING CONTRACT

(*Band leader's name*), representing (*the band's name*) hereby agrees to perform on (*date of performance*) between the hours of ______ and ______ at (*club's name*).

(*The club owner's name*) hereby agrees to pay the sum of $______ in U.S. currency for said performance(s) by (*date*) to (*band's name*). Check will be made out to _______________ if different from above band's name)

Special Requirements: (This is where you would list any requirements that either party might have, such as special lighting, dressing rooms, publicity, etc…) If you require an advance, state this on the contract, also.

Signed:	____________________ (band leader's name)	Signed:	____________________ (club owner's name)
	____________________ (leader's signature/date)		____________________ (owner's signature/date)
of the	____________________ (band's name)	of the	____________________ (club's name)

CHAPTER 4

ORGANIZING AND LEADERSHIP

BAND LEADER

The band must choose one person to be the leader, and the other members must respect that leader's direction. The leader is the one with the most knowledge of the business and has the best organizational skills. The leader is responsible for bookings, publicity and promotion, although he or she may assign some of the responsibilities to other members, depending on who is capable of doing the best job in that particular area.

Sometimes a family member or a dedicated friend will handle the bookings, especially if the band members all have day jobs and the relative or friend is available to receive and make calls. You would want someone with a pleasant phone personality and the ability to talk money and scheduling. Friends or relatives may not charge you, but if they do, a small fee might be worth it. If a buyer has to continuously hunt down a band, he will soon move on to another one. Don't let that happen to you. If the only time you can be reached is between 6 and 10 p.m., state that on your business card.

A business card should be considered an important investment, and as part of your promotional package, its value is incalculable. It should be creative without being cute or fussy; remember, it is a business card. It should include the band's name, a contact booking person, the type of music you perform (country, variety, soft rock, etc.) and an alternate number in case of emergencies.

TELEPHONES AND ANSWERING MACHINES

It is important to have an answering machine or voice mail. Your voice is your image, so when you use the telephone speak clearly and pleasantly. Keep messages short and speak with confidence.

Check the answering device when you arrive home, and return calls promptly. If you have an answering machine, make sure it's turned on before you leave the house.

Some people have car phones and some carry pagers; whatever works best in your situation, as long as the caller is able to reach you within a reasonable time.

PROMOTIONAL PACKAGE

Your promotional package, known as the promo, is your business folder. It represents who you are. Every band and every individual singer should have a professional-looking promo-package. I am a firm believer that good first impressions have a great impact on getting a job in any business. How you present yourself and your talent is vital to your success and is the marketing aspect of promoting your product—you and your band.

DEMO TAPE

Information about your talent, your image, and your qualifications go into the promotional folder. You capture this by getting the best local recording that you and your band can afford. The demonstration (demo) tape should not be too expensive if you prepare properly for it. Look in the yellow pages under "Studios" and make a list. Ask owners/managers of local music stores, record shops, and electronics stores for their opinions.

If you own a portable compact four-track cassette recorder, you can produce your own tape at home, if you mix it properly. If you need assistance with this, ask a sound engineer.

A four-track home recording would be acceptable for your first demo only, and only for the local club circuit. Most local studios use either an eight, 16, or 24-track. For your first demo, an eight-track tape is sufficient.

Call for prices and schedule an appointment to visit the studio. While there, ask to hear a tape the engineer has already produced. Listen for sound quality. An eight, 16 or 24-track studio usually has the latest in hi-tech equipment, so the quality will no doubt be acceptable.

Other than the obvious quality of sound, the most important element in a recording is the vocal mixing. Some studios, no matter how good the equipment, do not mix the vocal levels properly. I can only guess the reason. Most local studio engineers are musicians, not lead vocalists. They either mix the vocals at the same level as the other instruments, or drown them out entirely. For best results, listen to the vocals. If the vocals are clear and can be heard above the music, then you probably have a good mix. If not, ask the engineer to bring your vocals up. Listen to a recording of a professional singer and note that you can clearly hear every word in the song. That's what you want also.

When you have chosen your studio, have each song down pat before producing your demo tape. You probably should use your band on this tape, because club owners/managers want to hear the whole package you're asking them to pay for, not just the vocalist. Each member should pay an equal part of the expenses involved.

Four or five songs will be plenty for the demo. Pick your best work. Usually upbeat, high energy songs that are easy to dance to are encouraged, plus a good slow song or two for the lovers to dance to. If you have one song you feel compelled to sing (this can be an original if it's really good), include that.

If you are a country band, a country dance song would be a plus. Some examples are: "Boot Scootin' Boogie" (named after the song), "Super Love" (the Cowgirl Hustle dance), "Achy Breaky Heart" (the Achy Breaky dance), or Hillbilly Rock" (the Tush Push dance).

Be sure to write your band's name and two phone numbers on the tape. It could get separated from the package.

PICTURE

You'll need a good black-and-white 8 x 10 glossy photo of you and your band. Don't put a lot of money into this, because band members change and your own image will change as you grow. A black-and-white glossy can be used for newspapers, flyers and other promotional materials. A suggestion: to keep costs down, look for a photography student at a local college or perhaps a "moon-lighting" photographer from a local studio. Take the black-and-white photo to a print shop and have bulk copies run off at a reduced rate. Call your local printer for details. If you own a computer and scanner you might want to print off copies on a high quality printer.

The picture should project the band's image. Remember first impressions. What look are you going for? The picture will show whatever you are.

BIO

You will need a resume, commonly called a bio sheet. The bio is a short biographical listing of the band members, which instruments each one plays, what the band is collectively about, and the type of music it plays.

If one of the band members once traveled with a professional band, was part of a highly respected local band, or has had a record released, highlight that information. It could be just the reason you get your first gig.

You want to let the buyer know that yours is the new dynamite band that everyone is talking about. You are about energy, about excitement, you are people-oriented, and you are dependable. Then, be sure that you live up to your words at each performance.

As you enter and win major contests, you will want to include that information in your bio. In other words, include any notable recognition you and/or your group has achieved. (Examples included.) (see following pages for examples)

NAMING THE BAND

You will need a memorable name for your band. When choosing a name, be creative and make it work for you. Look at labels at the record shops and check out what other bands are calling themselves. Create your own band's identity—a name that says who you are. One local band that I know chose a weak name and they had trouble getting jobs. Then they changed to a name that stuck easily in promoters' heads, and believe it or not, they are booked all the time. Say, for example, you are an all-female band; if you called your band "Gentle Ladies" you might appear to be a group of low-key relaxed musicians, where as if you called your band "Wild & Sassy" you would tend to be thought of as fun-loving, exciting females ready to party.

When choosing a professional name for your group, check with your county and state businesses to find out if any other "fictitious" name already exists in the state you will be working in. When you are ready to branch out and perform in other states, check the Trademark Register at your local library, or talk to your attorney. You do not want to copy the same name, or the likeness of a name of any other group.

Your original band name is your trade name. Rights in trade names and trademarks are not covered under the copyright law. But it is a criminal offense to infringe on, imitate, or copy trade names or trademarks in most states. If you do want to register your name under a broader branch of law which has to do with unfair competition, you can write to The Government Printing Office, Washington, D.C. 20402 for a pamphlet about general information on trademarks.

A written agreement among the band members regarding the group's name might not seem important now, but it could be vitally important later. The group should decide who owns the professional name and what happens to the name when performers join or leave the group. A basic agreement should be typed up and signed by each member. If this isn't done, feelings can get in the way and a civil lawsuit may result. Treat this like any other business item now and save yourself some headaches later on.

The band name goes at the top of your bio. Once the bio is complete, the name has been selected, and the agreement has been written, one of the band members can type it on the computer and make copies on a quality printer.

Don't forget to get signatures on the band name agreement, but keep it out of your promo-package. All members get a copy of the agreement for their personal files.

Wild Love Rebellion

George Spieth *(Bassist)*

George first began performing music as a trumpet player in a school band. He taught himself to play the bass and is a veteran of the Richmond club scene. His early music interest was in hard rock, but he has been playing country music for the past three years. George just celebrated his first anniversary as the bassist and a backup vocalist for WILD LOVE REBELLION.

Robert Riley *(Drummer)*

Bob received formal training as a drummer when he was a teenager and was active in school bands. He has performed in numerous professional bands and is experienced in a wide variety of music genres. Bob has been the drummer for WILD LOVE REBELLION for six months.

Cathleen Clark *(Keyboardist)*

Cathy is formally trained and had her first experience preforming publicly in school bands. She was new to the club scene when she and her husband formed WILD LOVE REBELLION two years ago. In addition to playing the keyboard, Cathy provides lead and backup vocals and helps co-write original material for the band along with her husband, Paul.

Paul Clark *(Guitarist)*

Paul is a self-taught lead guitarist and has been performing professionally for many years. His early influences were primarily hard rock, but he is versatile in a wide variety of musical styles. He is the lead vocalist and guitarist for WILD LOVE REBELLION and also writes original material for the band.

If asked to describe their musical style, WILD LOVE REBELLION would classify it as "high-energy country." They perform every chance they get for private clubs and parties, nightclubs, and various public and charity events. They have been performing for approximately one year and are preparing to record their original work.

B LEAGUE CHAMPIONS

The B League Champions consist of five energetic and semi-normal teens that always look to rock the face off of those in attendance. Anthony Phillips and Adam Zuckerman were both in a band called *The Feat* before the B League era, and Andy Campbell, Danny Ubilla, and Brandon King were all in a group called *YBS.* Both bands had an addiction to rocking hard. The two bands happened to break up at the same time, and Anthony and Adam decided to join an already strapping force in Andy, Brandon, and Danny. The group decided on the name for their new band after seeing it on the back of a little league football jacket. Even though some members had played in bands together, and meshed very well, it wasn't until they combined the forces of both bands that their musical powers far exceeded anything any of them had accomplished before.

With driving percussion, melodically flooring bass lines, harshly serenading guitars, and keyboards that tip-toe into the foreground the B League Champions seem to have endless potential. The group blends pop-punk and indie-rock to create energetic yet musically solid songs. Most well known for their live shows, the B Leaguers always have the most energy on stage and it is evident that they have fun performing.

Anthony Phillips sings and plays keyboards. He is known for his *crazy antics* on stage, and for being *the ladies man* of the band His Keyboard parts add a light touch of finesse to the music. Adam Zuckerman plays the guitar and writes many lyrics that are poetic, but meaningful. The guitar parts he writes are both musically pleasing and easy to build on. Danny, *crazy fingers,* Ubilla also plays guitar. Although all the members are goofballs, Dan takes the cake while his guitar playing adds a subtle edge to any song. Brandon King is the *jumping* bass player and part-time singer for the band. His vocal harmonies and bass lines add a unique musical touch. Andy Campbell, another big fun-loving goofball, plays the drums and is a main source of the musical energy and drive of the band.

If you ask any member of the B Leaguer's band what they enjoy most about performing, they will tell you, *IT'S FUN.* Ask anyone who has ever heard the band play what they think and you will hear, *THEY ROCK.*

EQUIPMENT AND SONG LIST

An equipment list (instruments, PA system, and lights) and the song list (the songs and the keys you sing them in) should be included in your packet. These things are extremely important to a club owner/manager. You and the members of the band should keep up with the latest songs being played on the popular music stations. People prefer to dance to songs they know and like. (Originals can be thrown in, on occasion, after you have a following.) Keep a repertoire of old standards and add to that list as newer songs take their place.

A copy of the articles written about the group or any member of the group should be included in your promo package, as well as letters of recommendation you have received since you began performing. To get these: first, be sure there were no major problems with the equipment or performance. then ask the promoter, benefit organizer, or club owner/manager to write you a letter of recommendation. Once you have compiled several good recommendations, delete any old ones from your folder (unless it came from a highly respected promoter or person with business clout). You will want to keep the ones that reflect your best image.

FOLDER

Your promotional package is now complete. Paper clip your business card to the left pocket of the folder. People read from left to right and it will be the first noticeable item when the folder is opened. Place the picture inside the left pocket, so it too attracts the eye immediately. The bio sheet, equipment list, song list, and recommendations go in the right pocket of the promotional folder, along with the demo tape. There is no hard and fast rule about this; it just makes sense. Now you are officially ready for the real work—getting those bookings.

ABOUT BOOKINGS

Preservation, patience, and practicality are important in getting bookings. The most important of these three may be patience—patience to keep going no matter how tough it gets, yet at the same time being realistic about "when to hold them and when to fold them."

Whoever is in charge of bookings should a have list of the clubs, the promoters of local events, and the lodges (Moose, Elks, Legions and others) in your area. List the name of the organization, the contact person, the address and the phone number. For the clubs and lodges, look in the yellow pages, at ads in the entertainment section of the local newspapers, in your local entertainment publications, and flyers that other bands have posted around town. For the fairs, benefits, festivals, and other local events, ask your Chamber of Commerce, call the fair grounds, contact local benefit groups, ask your local radio station (Often a deejay emcees local events), scout the newspapers, and ask questions. Networking is vital in the music business.

Once your list has been compiled, ask who handles the bookings or the entertainment. Put that name on your list of potential bookings (clubs, lodges, and events). Call that person and tell him or her you would like to send a promo package for possible bookings. If the club is not already using a local disc jockey, send out your promo package immediately. Wait a week and place a follow-up call to verify the package was received. Ask if they have had the time to review it yet. Show real interest in wanting to perform at the establishment or event. Ask if you are being considered for a possible booking, but avoid being too aggressive. Ask if you may drop by in person. If the person doing the booking is still hesitant, ask if you could give him or her one free audition night other than a Friday or Saturday.

Remember, this is your business. If you use good practical marketing techniques, you will get bookings.

When you do get that booking, ask if you can set up your equipment on the afternoon of the performance. This will give you and your band the opportunity to do the sound checks appropriate for the size of the club, and you and your musicians will have time to relax before the performance.

Make another quick sound check when you arrive for the performance and you are ready.

Tell all of your family and friends where you will be performing and try to pack the place. Most clubs have a set fee they pay local bands, depending on experience, talent, and following. So don't forget the “make the customer happy theory.” Happy customers equal a happy club owner. Not to mention a happy you.

SUMMARY OF PART I

TO GET STARTED YOU WILL NEED:

- Talent
- The ability to develop your talent
- Organizing skills and leadership abilities
- A band and equipment
- To rehearse, rehearse, and rehearse some more
- A promotional package
- A few free practice performanccs
- A basic contract
- Bookings that pay for performance

Using this suggested method, you will probably fill your calendar fast. The more in demand you are, the more in demand you'll become. The more in demand you become, the closer you get to making that climb to the next level—branching out are the first steps, and they will form the basis of everything that will follow. Do yourself a favor and have this first phase of your career down pat before moving on. Once you accumulate a following, are in demand and feel that you are ready for a new challenge, it is time for you to start developing yourself and your act, and branching out into new territory. How much time you spend on the basics is entirely up to you and your band. It depends on your ambition, on how much you are willing to work at it, and how earnestly you want it. Some bands never move to the next phase, and that is all right for them. But if you are that special talent striving for superstar status, in two years of working hard in the right direction, you will be itching for a challenge and will be ready to move on to the next level.

 **NOTES** 

PART II

BRANCHING OUT

CHAPTER 5

♪

EXPOSURE AT THE NEXT LEVEL

Moving to this new level is very exciting. Your audiences will increase from a few hundred to a few thousand. Of course you will still book the clubs, lounges, lodges, and other smaller events. You will need to work during the cold spells and play the smaller jobs to keep your schedule full.

This will not be easy, but you need to keep growing and challenging yourself; you have worked very hard to get this far. You have talent, your band is musically sound, and it is time to move up and into new territory. Now your band will expect and want you, the lead singer, to develop your showmanship. You will start developing a style of your own, become more of an entertainer, and will even begin to sign autographs. There will be ups and downs, but it is important to stay focused on the positive.

It is at this point that you could use some help. Seek publicity.

PUBLICITY

Check with your local newspaper to see who would be willing to write an article on you and your band. Do what you can to generate publicity in local trade papers or band books in your area. It's up to you to create hype for yourself and your band. Here's where your local organizers come in handy—county fairs, festivals, special event shows. Get that first big job. Contact the right people and get on the program.

The promoter pays for publicity, and your name will be on posters, the radio, possibly on local television, on flyers, in brochures, and newspapers for miles around. You will probably be opening for a well known recording artist. This is an exciting possibility—be ready for it.

OPENING FOR A MAJOR ARTIST

Usually promoters, or buyers of talent, will supply sound and lights, but sometimes they will hire a group as the opening act if they also have the technical capabilities to provide the sound as well. At this time, it would benefit the group to upgrade its PA system to a 12 or 16 channel mixer. The financial gain will be greater, and the promoter saves money. A win-win situation for both.

Talk to promoters and find out what the requirements are when opening for a major artist. Then talk to your local music store manager about purchasing the best equipment for the best price you can get. Sometimes you will find good used equipment from bands that are splitting up. For information on this, contact your music sources. If promoters can get good sound and a great opening band for only a slight increase in budget, don't you suppose they would use it over an expensive sound company? I've seen it happen and I've used it myself.

If you are hired to provide sound, and your sound board operator has never run a medium-sized concert, hire a competent sound engineer from a company with a reliable reputation. A small to medium sound company with extensive experience will do a professional job, and for less money than the larger sound companies.

If you mess up the sound, you won't be working with that promoter again, and the major artist not only won't be happy to meet you, but he or she will likely refuse to work with you again. Try a few performances before offering to provide sound.

The promoter will tell you, or it will be written in your contract, when you should arrive the day of performance for sound checks. The sound engineer usually arrives early in the morning and stays throughout the day as musicians arrive for individual sound checks. The opening act should arrive an hour or two before the scheduled performance time (or earlier). This keeps the promoter happy and allows plenty of time to work out last minute details. Also, don't spend money on food until you determine whether the promoter arranges for catered meals for the cast and crew.

Once you have your contract, rehearse, rehearse, rehearse. The band has to be tight on every note, at every pause. The singer and the band should work out stage signals, what they mean and when to use them. It is vital to a smooth, professional-sounding performance that the band follows your lead.

When opening for a major act or artist, it is crucial to remember that the audience paid the big bucks to see the star of the show, not you. You are not a star yet, but you get the chance to work on developing to be one. Your job is to promote the headline act during your performance. Without the major artist, the show wouldn't exist and you wouldn't have the opportunity to perform in front of thousands. Your main function of being an opening act is to excite the audience, and make it easier for the main attraction to walk out and do a killer performance.

Isn't that satisfying? You are such a good sport: you entertain with all the energy you can muster, remind the audience of who they really came to see, smile, entertain, and excite them into wanting you to leave the stage so someone else can get the glory.

But for being such a good sport you get paid, you receive plenty of free publicity, you meet the major artists, have your picture taken with them, and have something substantial to put on your resume—not to mention the chance to make even more money by selling merchandise (tapes, photos, caps, buttons, bumper stickers, and t-shirts.) Sometimes you will be required to pay a small percent of merchandise sales to the venue, but other times you get to keep all the profits.

Another advantage of opening for a major act, or artist, is the opportunity to generate a larger following. As people stop at your table for merchandise or an autograph, give them a schedule of your monthly performances. Concerts are not the same as performing at a small club; it is okay to hand out schedules while performing at a larger venue, unless the promoter states otherwise.

Do everything you can to gain new followers. Perhaps a friend or fan will start a local fan club for your group and will collect names and addresses for you. Fan club leaders can be a big help. They send out the monthly newsletters, work the concession stand, promote you, and will put together a yearly social function as a way for you to build a stronger relationship between you and your fans. This is an excellent way to increase your following and start building hype. Be entertaining and get people to like you.

Once you are opening for major artists it is important to start developing your voice, style, and stage presence. You will also establish a band logo and add to your merchandise inventory.

LOGOS

Your logo is your group's trademark and includes the group's trade name. Trademarks do not fall under the copyright law.

Be as original in creating your logo as you were in naming your band. The logo is a visual description of who you are. so let the design tell the story. As in ownership of name, the same type of agreement between group members should be written and signed. Remember the headache theory—take care of business now, and there will be no headaches later.

MERCHANDISE

Look in the itemized section of your telephone directory for the type of merchandise you want to sell. For example: look under "Caps" and you will see the page number of each business pertaining to caps. Another good source are your local club owners; they buy merchandise. Call the businesses and get prices and schedules for having your band's logo imprinted on your caps and shirts. When you have your merchandise, ask the business person who imprinted your logo, a promoter, a club owner, or another band for a suggested retail price.

With the image of today's family scene so often referred to in the negative sense, it is remarkable that a group of songwriters and musicians so full of life and talent would be such professionals and family. That unique family is known all along the East Coast as DEMIN & LACE!

The family band members are: Wayne Bailey on acoustic guitar/singer, his wife Vickie as lead singer/back-up, their son Tory on guitar/drums/singer, and Wayne's brother Gregg on drums/singer. The other members of the DEMIN & LACE band are: Sam Lewis on bass guitar, Mark Bright on steel guitar, and Wes Holcomb on lead guitar/fiddle. The combination of this family and friends band is what makes this group so unique. Their friendship, combined with their musicianship projects the finest showmanship and professionalism in their performance.

The dedication and quality of their craft has kept DENIM & LACE in front of audiences for the past ten years. They have opened for many major recording artists: Garth Brooks, Reba McEntire, Ronnie Milsap, Ronnie McDowell, Waylon Jennings, Statler Brothers, Doug Stone, Mark Chestnut, Sawyer Brown, Juice Newton, Ricky Van Shelton, Ricky Scaggs, T Graham Brown, Mary Chapin-Carpenter, Marty Stuart, Exile, John Anderson, Shenandoah, Vince Gill, and others. They have performed before audiences ranging from a few hundred to over fifty thousand. DENIM & LACE treats all audiences the same. They perform each show with the utmost of quality, energy, enthusiasm, and respect. They are a real crowd pleaser!

Book DENIM & LACE and let them please your audience with their Top 40 country, rock-a-billy, traditional country, and country-rock style. They don't just sing and play – DENIM & LACE entertains!

For superior, energetic, fun-filled entertainment at your fairs, clubs, lounges, lodges, banquets, receptions, company picnics, wedding receptions, and other functions you need the band that provides it all – Music, Sound, Lights, and Excellence: DENIM & LACE.

DENIM AND LACE

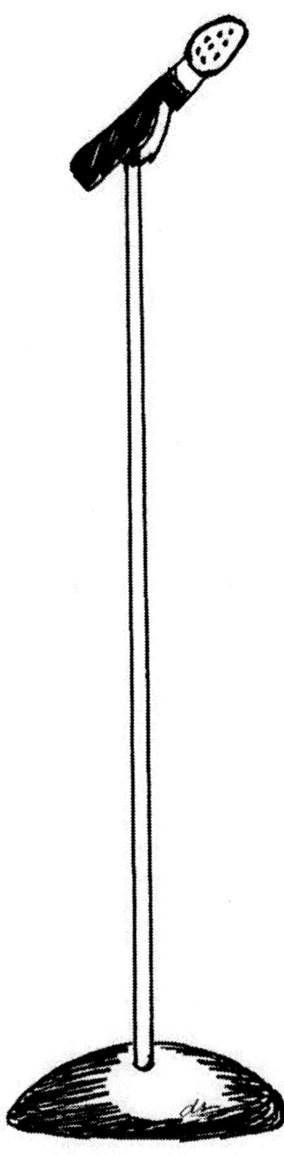

CHAPTER 6

STYLE AND VOICE

UNIQUE SOUND

What is style? It is your own unique sound. I've heard it referred to as "having 'it'" or as "being different," but what does that mean to the aspiring singer? Think of it this way: when you turn on the radio and a new song is playing, can you tell right away who belongs to the voice? If you can't, then that singer sounds like everyone else (or close to it) and doesn't have a unique sound of his or her own. In the first two measures of a song I know it's Reba McEntire, Wayne Newton, Willie Nelson, Shaina Twain, Lyle Lovette, or Tracey Chapman (to name a few) in the first eight beats. They have a special sound—their own style of singing.

Your singing style is your sound, your uniqueness, your ability to express in a certain way—a way that only you can. How many times in Winchester, Virginia, where Patsy Cline grew up, have I heard, "You should hear this new singer; she sounds just like Patsy Cline."

First of all, I don't believe anyone could really duplicate Pasty Cline; she was one of a kind. Secondly, sounding like another singer is okay when you're starting out, but it would be your demise now. Unless, of course, you want to make a living as an impersonator.

Loretta Lynn once told a singer friend of mine that she sang "too pretty". What she was probably saying is that the singer was not using her own unique sound.

Most overly trained voices are "too pretty". For instance, most theme park singers have to perform in this type of blended style. These trained singers usually know how to work the voice, but because they have to sing a certain way, they sometimes have a difficult time adjusting to being a lead singer in a band. Notice I said "most"; there are always exceptions. For the serious non-exceptions, the ones with determination and willingness to work, the adjustment will come.

Your style should be natural and believable. If you "put on" a style, it will come across as phony and people won't accept it.

Michael Twitty might sing a medley of his dad's—the late great legend of country music, Conway Twitty—but he sings in his own style, feels what he sings, and delivers a believable emotion.

YOUR INSTRUMENT

You develop your own unique sound through your instrument—your voice. Many singers go a life time, and do quite well financially, but never give much thought to the most important part of their careers—their instrument. It is a good idea to start right now, in the beginning of your career, to learn how to take care of and use this instrument properly. If you understand how your body works, use it correctly, and take care of it, your voice will have longevity. Otherwise, over a period of years, you may have to take time out for a throat operation or an extended rest of the vocal cords.

How does your instrument work and how is it unique to you? The diaphragm is a double, dome-shaped muscle of respiration that is positioned in the center of your body. It separates the top half of your body from the bottom half. It supports and controls the lungs. For this reason it is a good idea to exercise your legs and arms before each performance. This "warm-up" exercise will help your circulation. Good circulation will help your muscles to relax. Relaxed muscles will greatly improve your singing voice. Also, singing with the aid of the diaphragm will help your resonators select particular pitches.

The resonators are shaped structures that reinforce the ranges of sound. They are the cavities of the mouth, throat, nose and larynx. If they are not used properly, you could have a high pitched nasal sound. Most singers can't get away with a "too nasal" sound, Willie Nelson being one of the few exceptions. The reason it works for him is because he is one of a kind. His ability to work his style of voice with his unique guitar-playing style is what sets him apart from everybody else.

The larynx is the uppermost part of the trachea, the part that includes the vocal cords (the voice box). The vocal cords are two small pairs of tough elastic folds of connective tissue (vocal bands). Pulsations of the vocal cords create sound from the voice. The opening between the vocal cords is called the glottis. But what does this have to do with your unique sound?

COMBINATION OF SOUND

There are four fundamental human voice characteristics or attributes: loudness, pitch, duration and quality. Voices are associated with individuals that make sounds. The sounds and pitch can be altered to reflect any number of people, but when the loudness, resonance, and pitch are combined at the same time, it is unique to individuals. The combination can be improved on to develop your particular sound—your style of singing. The listener picks up your particular combination of sound through a process called timbre.

Timbre is how the ear recognizes and identifies different voices. The timbre is the distinctive quality given to a sound by its overtones. Your voice has its own distinctive overtones and is what you will become known for; how other people hear your unique combination of sound. You will have your own energy level of distribution. The vibrations in your voice initiate the tone and the manner to which resonators respond. Sometimes it is difficult to listen to a voice with too much vibrato. Dolly Parton gets away with it beautifully—it's her own combination of sounds and she knows how to work with it for best results. But for most of us, it's best to avoid too much vibrato.

Tones are multidimensional and are characterized by pitch, loudness, duration and the quality of timbre. Volume increases with the intensity of the tone and varies with the frequency of the tone.

When singing through a microphone, let the microphone work for your volume. Don't over-work your voice; it isn't necessary to holler when singing into a microphone. The volume is controlled by the sound engineer.

Volume is measured in decibels and relates to the amount of air you have in your lungs. You are in control of the force and energy of your voice by regulating the volume—the loudness or softness, emphasizing for feelings and emotions in your songs.

The sound engineer monitors the audio levels based on your natural singing voice. At sound checks, make sure your microphone is set so that your voice can be heard clearly, a little above the other instruments. This is very important. Have you ever watched a singer whose lips are moving, but you have no idea what it is you are supposed to be hearing? If this ever happens to you, have a serious talk with your sound engineer.

You may think it isn't important to know how your instrument works because—you've been told—everyone likes how you sound already. Everyone? I bet you haven't talked to the head honchos in the music business industry. You can be like everyone else and struggle all of your life or you can develop you to the point that someone will have to take notice. The music business is just that—a business. The business looks for someone who is polished, ambitious, creates hype, and has a unique quality of sound. You will be their product—the money maker. The more you understand about the industry and how your instrument works, the greater your chances are to succeed. It takes tenacity to survive it

CHAPTER 7

STYLE AND STAGE

DEVELOPING HYPE

Now down to the fun stuff—your stage performance. This is what separates you from all the other achievers. If you're used to being on stage and feel right at home, doesn't that give you an advantage? Yes, that's the first step—not to let the stage intimidate you. But there is so much more to it. Do you want to be an average singer or do you want to be an entertainer—one that the audience can't stop talking about? To do that, you must create hype, because hype equals excitement. You have to get the audience excited about you. Anyone can sing to them. For example, Ronnie McDowell is one of the best concert and club entertainers I've been associated with. He involves the audience and makes them feel as if it is their show, not his. He doesn't just talk and joke with them, he makes them part of the show, People love it. He creates hype.

THE AUDIENCE

One very important aspect of being a good entertainer is to know who your audience is and work with them. Adapt your performance to their age, educational, and social levels. Be prepared to cope with the unexpected: infants crying, airplanes flying overhead, microphone problems, sudden weather changes, your act being cut short, your name mispronounced, children running up on stage, or people interrupting you for an autograph. If any of these annoying things happen, keep calm and handle them with a smile and a sense of humor. Your promoter, stage hand, or security will step in to be the tough guy if that's necessary. You stay likeable. If your name is pronounced incorrectly while you are being introduced, wait until after your first song and you are acknowledging the audience. Repeat who you are clearly a couple of times. "Hi everybody, It is so nice to see you at the—(major artist's name) show. We are the—(your band's name) band and we're so excited to be here. I am—(your name).

Keep it short and get into entertaining. Excite them, get them riled up, and keep it building until you finally announce the one they paid to see. When that artist walks out to face the audience, the audience should be screaming and cheering. The artist will usually mention your name and give you credit for a job well done. Let the artist walk out to a silent crowd and you can forget the recognition, and perhaps any chance of opening for that artist again. This is why it is so important to know your audience.

THE POWER TO INFLUENCE

> …Music is a higher revelation
> than all…wisdom and philosophy.
> -Beethoven

Music is a powerful art: it can create mood swings, influence how much or how little one eats, keeps people active or puts them to sleep, and it can influence people's well being. That's powerful stuff, and you have the power to be part of this influence on others. How you influence audiences will become vitally important to the outcome of your career. There have actually been studies done on the influence of music upon human physiological functions and the mind. People react to music in ways they might not ordinarily act.

> —The licensed medium for bawling in
> public. Things too silly or sacred
> to be uttered in ordinary speech.
> -Oliver Herford

Emotion is a psychological expression. It is the way individuals feel and react to your music. Watch people's reactions to different types of music—dance, march, popular, rap, classic, country, blues, jazz, lullaby, ballad, opera, etc. Notice how you feel when listening to the various types of music. It is important to anticipate how people will react during your performances.

There are many types of people: the physically, emotionally, or mentally handicapped; individuals with behavioral problems; special interest groups; military personnel; political people in power;

professionals; super intellectuals; and artistically talented people. Know which type you are performing for and adapt to their interests. Next, take into consideration the predominant gender of the audience, its personality, ethnic origin, age, type of worker (white/blue collar), attitude, and religious beliefs. Is this audience noisy and active or quiet and passive? There is much more to performing than just singing in front of a group of people. You need wisdom as well as talent.

The smaller the audience is, the more personalized you can be. Large crowds tend to think of entertainers as being bigger than life and they like flash, glamour, and a lot of energy. They also like special effects, props, and variety in a show—they paid big bucks and they want it all.

Don't let any of this intimidate you. Do your homework and give the best performance you have the ability to give. Take each performance and use it as a learning device for the next one.

One more thing about audiences: you never know who might be in one. It could be your step to fame. So just because an audience is small doesn't mean it isn't important.

THE SONG

Every song you sing should project some type of emotion that moves others. If you sing every song with some kind of emotion and sincere feeling, then you will move your audience. Sing with real enthusiasm. If you are going to sing a love song, then sing as though you are deeply in love—sing it sweetly and tenderly. If you are going to sing a gut-wrenching, tear-jerking ballad, then sing like you are hurting—feel the pain of the moment.

If you are going to sing an upbeat song, then act upbeat—smile, move with that beat, feel that happiness, and project that energy to your audience. Move them, make them feel what you are feeling, and do it each and every time. It doesn't matter how much money someone puts up, if the audience doesn't react, that money is wasted. Many singers never learn this. That's why there are so few superstars. Audiences these days are sophisticated and they require a certain level of sophistication from their entertainers.

A song's lyrics have to mean something. If you are good at telling stories and writing poetry, try writing lyrics. Make the lyrics meaningful and sing the type of songs you do best. If you can't feel what you are singing, then listen to your inner self and don't sing that song. When Patsy Cline started out, she sang a variety of different songs, but it wasn't until her manager suggested that she specialize in singing ballads that her career really took off. Pasty could belt out a ballad like no other and her music is still the top of the line—long after the fatal plane crash that took her young life. Patsy believed that if you can't sing with emotion, you shouldn't sing at all.

The song is the most important key to having a hit record. If you have a song with a great hook—something simple like "Achy Breaky Heart," by Billy Ray Cyrus, or John Anderson's "Just a Swingin'"—you'll get instant recognition. A hook is the melodic line that people remember. It is usually in the chorus and is repeated throughout the song. A hook can come from anywhere. Remember the hook "Don't Worry, Be Happy"? Something so simple caught on like wildfire. Bobby McFerrin was standing on the side of the road by his disabled car when another car full of young people rode by. One of them hollered out the window, "Don't worry, be happy." That became the hook to a song that was an overnight success.

How do you know what's a hit? People have pondered that question for years. In my opinion, a hit is a record that causes the collective mass listeners to feel something. They cannot stop humming it, singing it, playing it on an instrument, or dancing to it. Listen to today's hit songs and study them until you can recognize the hook and how the music makes you feel—and why.

ACTING TECHNIQUES

Developing your stage presence is necessary when you have reached this phase of your singing career. How do you develop stage presence? As an entertainer you have to be all things to all people, and it is your responsibility to see that the audience is having a good time. Even a highly sophisticated audience likes a good laugh or a dramatic moment.

A suggestion which will greatly improve your performance and stage presence is to take a beginner's acting class. But you do not want to be an actor, you want to be a singer. Why do you need acting lessons? You don't, if you are happy being average. But acting helps develop emotion, feeling, and interacting with people. Celine Dion said she gave her heart to the "Titanic" theme by "finding the actress within". She believes singing is acting.

Theatre games and the fundamentals of acting are excellent types of classes for the beginner. In theatre games you will learn to create, to feel, to move others, and to act by yourself.

In the fundamentals of acting you will learn how to interact with other performers, you will strengthen your memory skills, and will learn how to deliver (speak dialogue) with confidence. Most high schools have a drama department and some colleges and universities offer acting for non-acting majors. Another alternative is to join a community theatre group. If joining is too time consuming, then perhaps the high school drama coach or the community artistic director would consider coaching you for a small fee.

There are other good reasons to know something about the art of acting. They are: about music videos, perhaps a music movie role, performing on television, and other media events. If you are a naturally tense person, a dance movement class or a choreography coach would be beneficial for both your performance and music videos. Once you have mastered the art with confidence, apply your acting to your singing.

THE PERFORMANCE

The lead singer/entertainer isn't the only part of the show. The musicians should showcase their particular instruments during each performance. When opening for a major artist, the opening act can last from a half-hour to an hour. As a rule, the major act can take between forty-five minutes to ninety minutes. By showcasing the musicians, you get a chance to rest your body, especially your vocal cords. It also adds variety to the show. This may vary, depending on venue, promoter, number of acts, and the type of show.

You have your act together—you are full of energy, you sing with feeling and emotion, your musicians have their instrumental pieces ready, and the band knows your stage signals. You can't wait for the day of performance. Relax and stay grounded. The most important thing to do now is—what else?—practice, practice, and practice.

If you deliver a good show, you'll add fans and sell merchandise. If you have a tape and one person buys it, you can bet that several other people will hear it. Your fans will generate others to be interested in you. They, in essence, become your promoters.

If permitted, and this is a big if, try to get someone to video tape your act so that you and your band can critique the show later. One caveat: video and tape recorders are usually not permitted in the audience during a performance by a major act. Ask the promoter if one would be allowed during your performance only. Explain why you want it. If the answer is no, then tape a good rehearsal.

Never blame the audience for a bad show. It is your responsibility to do the best entertaining job you can, it's the sound engineer's job to provide quality sound, and it is the promoter's responsibility to take care of the rest. It is the audience's play time and they don't deserve blame if things don't go as well as you'd expected or hoped.

A great performance is one that grabs and holds the audience's attention and leaves them wanting more. In other words, kick the show off with a lot of energy, offer a variety of entertainment, involve your audience, and end the show with a bang. From beginning to end, it's energy, emotion and feeling, and more energy.

COSTUMES

To be a total entertainer you should look the part. Audiences want you to look like an entertainer. They'll take you more seriously, and you should care what they want.

For a country act, men can get away with the jeans look more easily than women can. If a woman wears jeans she will have to add flair: great western boots, a dressy jacket, or a combination of western and Indian wear. Willie Nelson gets away with old jeans and tee shirts, but even he adds uniqueness with his long hair and head bands. Clint Black gets away with the jeans because he is a Roy Rogers type (jeans and westerns go together). But Clint wears just the right hat or just the right jacket, which sets him apart from the others. Most of the country male singers do look great in jeans and jackets, but there are times when even they will want to change their style of dress for a particular look. Then there is Madonna—someone who changes her look and costume so often that the audience is fascinated by her. I'm not sure if Modonna does this as a gimmick for her act, or if she just finds repetition too unchallenging.

Rockers sometimes "dress down", or wear little clothing in order to show skin. Most Rap artists wear big, baggy clothing which sets them apart as a particular group of entertainers—even so, they create their own wardrobe style that signifies who they are.

It's best to change costumes if you are performing two shows in the same day—a day costume and a flashier one for the evening show.

Some singers already have a different enough look to begin with, and their style works for them—K.D. Lang and Cher come to mind. They both have their own style of dress, which clearly identifies them as individuals. (They both have kept the same hair styles over the years, as well.) If you have a strong identity and it matches your particular personality, then that's your style and you shouldn't change it. As long as you perform your greatest and the audience reacts positively toward you, nothing else matters. Be who you are and build on it. Try to include colors that highlight your features and skin tone. This is especially important when dealing with the electronic media.

CHAPTER 8

THE MEDIA

THE PRINT MEDIA

When dealing with the media, it is important to keep a positive relationship. They have deadlines, so respond quickly. Learn to communicate well with the press—they can help or hurt your career. Use them, but don't abuse them. When used properly, the media can create and build hype for you.

When you have a big event planned, send the media a press kit. It should include a definite purpose: to obtain news coverage of a public event, to create interest in a project, or simply to release important information. Remember the who, what, when, where, and why. The press kit should include a contact name, address, and telephone number for you or your group. State the date you want your news released to the public: "For release on (specific date)." Include: your bio, photograph, press pass, instructions on where to park and what part of the building to enter, any pamphlets, brochures, or other pertinent promotional material. Place the entire package in an attractive cover. (It is okay to use a two-pocket folder.)

Call press contacts ahead of time and tell them what you will be sending. While you have them on the phone, verify their name and address and add them to your file.

RADIO INTERVIEWS

Be professional and positive. Your voice is your image, so speak clearly and slowly in a relaxed normal tone. Never interrupt your host or other guests. If you are being left out of the conversation and want to participate in a conversation between host and another guest, motion with your hand or wait for them to make their point, then make yours. Always be courteous. If you have to sneeze or cough, don't do it into the microphone. Muffle the sound with your hand or clothing. When you do speak over the air, change your voice pitches.

If you speak in a monotone voice you will probably lose listeners, and will not be invited back to that station.

TELEVISION INTERVIEWS

Be prepared. Know the name of the show, the booking producer's name and phone number, where to report and when, the topic of conversation you will be discussing, the name and address of the station, the show's format—taped interview or live show, how much time is budgeted for you, who the other guests are (if any), and your interviewer's name. Ask if you will be reading from a prompter copy (a mechanical device that magnifies a typed script and allows you to read while looking directly at the lens of the camera) or ask if you should bring your own visuals or props. If you bring your own, be sure to arrive early to allow the visual engineer time to set it up. Make a checklist and confirm your schedule the day before the interview.

Arrive 15 to 30 minutes early (earlier if you bring props) and relax. Give security or the receptionist your name and the booking producer's name. Make sure your name is spelled correctly. At a small station you'll usually wait in the lounge. At a major network you will be seated in a waiting room (called the green room) and will be asked to sign a release form saying that you won't sue them for anything that is said about you during air time. Because of this, make sure that you tell the producer ahead of time if there is any subject that you don't want discussed.

Be personable. Look friendly and smile. Unless requested to do so, look into the eyes of the interviewer, not at the camera. If you will be looking into the camera, pretend it's your friend and talk to it.

Dress appropriately and avoid flashy jewelry. There are certain colors that clash with the color spectrum of the camera, while others complement: black and white stripes or checks clash, solid white could give you a ghostly appearance, and solid black does not work well with a dark background. Most other colors would be appropriate. It is best to check with the particular studio for advice.

BEING PHOTOGRAPHED

Some tips on being photographed are: Use black and white for newspapers and color for national magazines; wear the right colors for best results for tv news and video-taped pieces; during an action shot, prolong the wave or movement, and don't face the camera directly—advance your shoulder slightly and gently tilt your head. (A good photographer avoids head on shots with both ears showing.) Also, present your best side whenever possible. Make sure to take off your sun glasses and don't squint at the sun. When you are in a group photo, avoid a "too busy" background and stay to the middle of the group. That way, if the picture gets chopped, you won't be cut out. If you are a fairly short person then try to stand in the front row. If you can't stand in the front, stay out of the way of heads and hats.

Unless told otherwise, always smile and give the appearance that you are a friendly person.

CHAPTER 9

HEALTH AND THE PERFORMANCE

TAKING CARE OF YOURSELF

Now that your schedule is demanding, you can not afford to get sick. If you get too tired, you will start making mistakes. If you get to the point of exhaustion, you may say or do something that could hurt you later in your career. You will need to appear in control. Be relaxed and stay calm. Let someone else handle debates. You don't want to become a workaholic too early on, or you'll burn out and become discouraged with the thing you once loved—singing. Whenever you can, take a break and do absolutely nothing.

When you reach the point in your career where you are shaking hands a lot, it would be wise to wash your hands before touching your face and especially before eating. Try to avoid contact when others have colds and are sneezing or coughing. Singers should avoid the temptation to smoke, over-indulge in alcoholic beverages, and using drugs. They all can affect your health, and may hinder your performances.

EXERCISE

Exercise before performing, especially your arms and legs. Walking is the best form of exercise, so try to set aside some walking time; it reduces stress and tension. If your performance is a particularly long one, move around while on the stage.

FOODS AND DRINKS

Eating the right foods will help your energy level, your attitude, and your alertness. Fruits, veggies, legumes and grains can provide all the protein, carbohydrates and calories you need to stay healthy. Before a performance, consider eating a slice of lemon to cleanse the vocal cords. Hot tea with honey will relax a swollen throat. A piece of fruit or a cup of yogurt can give you a quick boast when you're feeling tired.

Drink water throughout the day to avoid dehydration and having a dry mouth and throat. Avoid caffeine, especially before performances, it can constrict the blood vessels. Soft drinks and chocolate can make you feel bloated, and negatively acts on the allergies. Alcohol may make you feel relaxed, but it is actually a depressant; the effects are exacerbated under hot stage lights; Don't drink before and during performances, or during breaks. Save the alcohol for after-performance celebrations, if you must, but drink in moderation. Don't let members of your crew drink either, especially if they will be driving after the performance; you could be held accountable.

STRESS

Stress can work on your immune system and make you susceptible to colds and viruses. If you feel stress building and your schedule is full, then learn to delegate the smaller tasks to others.

If the other members of the group are also feeling the pressure, then it may be time to ask for help. For instance, you could hire an outside agency to handle bookings. There are local or regional booking agencies who can get you bookings out of your area. Look in the telephone directory of the largest city nearest you.

Do not sign an exclusive contract. If the agency has a great reputation for signing artists, you might want to sign exclusively, but not for longer than one year. Local and regional agencies usually book clubs and dance halls. Check with the club owners for references.

Keep your career goals to yourself, because there is the possibility that if an agency thinks you might not be around long, they might not get you the best jobs. On the other hand, if you are a better than average group and the agency finds you easy to book, they might not be concerned how long you stay. After all, 10 percent of a lot of gigs can add up quickly.

If you do sign with an agency that books you a lot of performances, be fair. Once the agency books you into a new venue—one you couldn't find on your own—don't go behind the agency's back and re-book yourself into that venue. If you do, you'll probably be dropped from that agency.

Consider hiring someone to work the concession stand with you. They sell while you give autographs and talk to your fans. Give the person a percentage of the merchandise sales, usually 10 percent.

Hiring people to do other jobs might save your sanity and will allow you to do what you love to do best—sing. You will still be in control of your career, but will not be as stressed out. Keep a sense of humor and accept growth as a positive career move. Be honest with yourself; do you really want this for your life? If the answer is yes, then remove the stress and work on how you want to be remembered in years to come—as a deserving superstar. But if the answer is no, then be fair to yourself and give it up.

 **NOTES** 

CHAPTER 10

COMPETITIONS

EARLY ON

If you want to enter every little contest that comes along when you are just beginning your career, then do it. It will give you a good feel for competition and if you lose, it will teach you how to handle possible rejection early in your career. Learn from the experience, and stay positive. Congratulate the winner and move on with your development.

If, after winning several contests, you find yourself in demand for performances, select only those contests with real incentive: heavy competition, money, a chance to perform at a larger event, or one that you would be proud to put in your promotional package. This type of competition is one that is sponsored by large companies such as True Value, Coca Cola, Budweiser, etc. Check with your local radio station to find out how and where to enter; some stations co-sponsor.

NATIONAL

Once you've developed your showmanship, have your own unique style, and can afford to travel, you might want to enter contests at a national level. Consider the following:

DOLLYWOOD COMPETITIONS

The Rising Star Talent Competition runs from June 25 - July 1, each year, at the Grand Hotel in Pigeon Forge, Tennessee. The categories for the auditions include single or group vocalists, dancers, instrumentalists, comedians, and others. The contestants are selected through regional competitions in approximately nineteen cities, and the national winners from each category are hired at Dollywood and the Dixie Stampede. There is a small fee for entering. For information on how to enter the regional competitions write to:

Rising Star Talent Productions
PO Box 30925
Gahanna, Ohio 43230
(740) 855-7720

There is an annual talent show at the Smoky Mountain Jubilee Theater in Pigeon Forge, held in November. The first forty applicants are selected to showcase. This talent show mostly features singers, but if you are exceptional in other categories you will not be overlooked. For more information and an application send a Self-addressed-stamped envelope to:

Attention: Elmer Dreyer
Smoky Mountain Jubilee
PO Box 1316
Pigeon Forge, Tennessee 37863
(423) 428-1836

BRANSON

Each year starting in April and running through November, a talent coordinator hosts a showcase on the last Sunday of every month at the Barbara Fairchild Theatre. This showcase gives amateurs a chance to perform on stage in Branson. There is a small donation required. All proceeds benefit Youth Life, an organization which helps teenagers in trouble. The showcase is informal and you never know who might be sitting in the audience Contestants sometimes have the opportunity to perform, for pay, at Branson's night spots. This showcase has brought music business people from around Branson and as far away as Los Angeles.

To apply, send a non-returnable audio or video tape, a photograph and your bio/resume. A talent committee will review your tape/video, and if chosen to perform, the talent coordinator will contact you for availability and scheduling. When this happens be confident and be prepared. Send promo-package to:

ATTN: Talent Showcase
3115 West Highway 76
Branson, MO 65616
(800) 494-2272

If you believe that you are ready to enter, then do it. If you are not selected at first, you will be better prepared for next year. You will know what is expected and will have a full year to work on any weaknesses. If you want to be recognized by the best, you have to be the best. Get help if and when you need it—from the vocal coach, the choreographer, any professional who will help you with weaknesses in you or your act.

NASHVILLE

In Mid-October through November, Nashville's Opryland Productions sponsors an annual talent search in various cities across the United States. If selected, you will be paid a competitive salary each week of performance. The salary is based upon production and skill level. They look for singers, featured performers, dancers, actors/specialty performers, instrumentalists, stage managers, and technical personnel. The open-call auditions are for casting performances at the: Alabama Theater, in Mytle Beach, South Carolina; the General Jackson showboat, in Nashville, Tennessee; Governor's Palace, in Pigeon Forge, Tennessee; the Mercury and the Century for Celebrity Cruise, Inc.; and for other future performances.

But you don't have to wait until the open-call to show your talent. Opryland Productions accepts videos of performers and resumes of stage managers and technical personnel throughout the year. For video and open-call audition requirements contact:

Opryland Productions
Creative & Entertainment Services
2802 Opryland Drive
Nashville, TN 37214
(615) 871-5600

Or call the Opryland Production voice-recorded hot-line at: (800) 947-8243. You can browse their website: lstegner@oprylandusa.com

Each September, Opryland Productions holds auditions for children for the Nashville Christmas show.

BLUEGRASS

It would be difficult to mention country music without giving at least some mention to bluegrass and Bill Monroe. Born September 13, 1911 as William Smith Monroe, in Rosine, Kentucky, Bill became known as the father and founder of a new kind of sound. This sound became known as bluegrass music, named after his Bluegrass Boys Band. Bill Monroe became a member of the Grand Ole Opry in 1935, and performed there until his death in 1996.

Because of him, a new type of music was created and out of it came bluegrass competitions. An annual bluegrass competition for the National Championship for Country Musician Beginners is held in July, just a few miles outside of Nashville. For more information, write to:

Old-Time Fiddlers Jamboree
P.O. Box 64
Smithville, TN 37166
(615) 597-8500

BEWARE

As a beginning singer, you will want to be cautious about people who call you on the telephone and say they want to record you, or ads in the newspaper that say a contest will be held in your area and you should call the 800 number.

When someone calls you, an unknown singer, on the telephone and says they have heard you sing, that you have real talent, and they would like to produce you in Nashville, listen carefully. They might be saying they will produce a record of you in Nashville only if you agree to pay them a sum of money; they may ask for as much as a few thousand dollars. They tell you if they produce you, they will distribute your record to the radio stations and try to get you on the charts. They may get you on the charts, usually at the lower end of the Independent (Indie) Record Label Charts.

The Independent Record Labels have achieved reputable recognition in the business, and there is a slim possibility that if your song catches on, it could climb higher on the charts—but it is unlikely. The caller guarantees you nothing else. He or she can't even guarantee you that your money will be used solely for promoting you. Most of the time the person calling has another artist he or she is trying to promote. Budgets are probably limited and additional financing is needed. What an easy way to increase the budget—calling unsuspecting hopefuls. You will get something for your money, but as a rule, it won't be what you had hoped for.

Also, every so often your home town newspaper will run an ad for Nashville contests at a location near you. The contest promoter may charge large entry fees or ask you to sell a lot of tickets. The winner (usually the one that sells the most tickets, and sometimes any one that has the money to travel) gets a recording (and sometimes a performance at some club or lounge room) in Nashville. You will get no promotion or distribution for your tape of two or three songs. The idea is that you sell as many tickets to the competition as you can. The competition host realizes that your friends and relatives will want to watch you compete. I mention Nashville because I have first-hand knowledge of what I write; however, the same scenario could happen in other types of music as well. Many aspiring singers have been disappointed, and many a dream has been squelched by these practices. Sometimes winners even leave their jobs and move to Nashville, only to move back home a few weeks later.

So before entering contests make sure that you understand the guidelines for the competition, and check with the Better Business Bureau in the area where the competition originates. If you still want to enter, then do it with open eyes. Usually, if you are the winner, you will have to pay your own round trip transportation and for your own living arrangements.

Before accepting recordings for pay, have an experienced person talk to the party in question. Find out exactly what you will get for your money, and ask for specific details to be put in writing.

Another type of newspaper ad is where an organization entices you to call an 800 or 900 number for more information on an area of the entertainment industry you may have an interest in, and then charges your telephone number, even if you didn't request the information you heard on the recording. Also, be careful about giving out too much information on the internet. Try to become as educated as possible about the different ways people can "trick" you. Every organization is not out to scam you, but please just be aware that it really does exist.

CHAPTER 11

TOURS

After you have performed at a few large events, proved that you are one pretty terrific act, and perhaps won a national competition, it's time to move to another challenge—touring. Two popular tours are the college tours and the USO overseas tours.

COLLEGE TOURS

Because young people buy tapes and compact discs, this is a good way to increase your following. Make sure you know your audience. What would the college kids laugh at? What is too serious to talk about? What type of songs do they like? The best way to know what college students like is to ask them. Do a marketing survey at college campuses, or ask your college friends. Get an understanding of who they are and what they are about. Attend a concert they would attend, and watch their reactions. After your first couple of performances you'll get better at it, but be prepared so you won't bomb.

The way to get on the college tour circuit is to market your talent at their annual convention. For information write to:

National Association
for Campus Activities
13 Harbison Way
Columbia, SC 29212

NACA is a talent and education market place. The director of convention and member services can be reached at (803) 732-NACA and 800-845-2338. Or browse their website: www.naca.org

OVERSEAS TOUR

An excellent way to start performing in other countries is through the USO overseas tours. They are handled through the Armed Forces Professional Entertainment Office (AFPEO) in Alexandria, Virginia.

The overseas tours include professional and non-professional entertainers. You must be entertaining and amusing, and must be able to lift the spirits of the armed forces stationed at remote and isolated sites throughout the world. Can you help them forget their problems for awhile? To do this work, you must be sincere and highly dedicated.

The AFPEO looks for groups with a high degree of quality and showmanship. The groups are highly screened, auditioned, and interviewed. The most successful groups perform a fast-paced, variety show—current pop, rock, R & B, country, and other formats.

You will not be paid a salary, but you will receive transportation and a daily living allowance for room and board.

You must be at least eighteen years of age and be able to travel without an escort, unless the escort is one of the performers selected.

For an application and requirements write to:

Director of Celebrity Entertainment
USO World Headquarters
601 Indiana Avenue N.W.
Washington, D.C. 20004
(202) 610-6480

CRUISE SHIPS

Travel agencies have access to the names of Cruise Lines. Call and ask for the telephone numbers of as many names as they are willing to assist you with. I have selected a name, at random, to use as an example. The number for the Royal Caribbean is 1-800-327-2056. When you call, you'll get a recording. Stay on the line and a representative will speak with you. Ask him for the on-board human resource department telephone number. The Royal Caribbean on-board human resource department number is (305) 982-2699. A recording will tell you to send a full resume and a cover letter stating the position you want. Because you are seeking employment as an entertainer you would also send a promo-package and a cover letter to:

Royal Caribbean Cruises
1050 Caribbean Way
Miami, Florida 33132
ATTN: Shipboard Human Resources

You have to be a dynamite act before you will be selected to entertain on a cruise ship. It is usually difficult to get on the entertainment program list, as the waiting lists are long. Cruise ships hire through talent agencies and by direct mailing from individual artists. But, because you have prepared yourself for all audiences, you will send in your promo-package anyway. If selected, you will be scheduled for an audition. If there are no openings available at the time you audition, your package will be placed in the file for possible future bookings. If you really want that cruise ship job, follow-up by writing occasional professional inquiries.

OTHER TOURS

There are other tours for long distance performing in the United States if you are willing to look for them: call a car, truck, boat, or motor coach distributor and ask for their headquarter's number. Ask how to reach their entertainment director. When you have reached that person, ask if they are accepting promotional packages for sponsorship. A particular branch of the national organization will act as your sponsor and you would work at their rallies for pay and expenses. If they agree to you sending a package, send it out immediately. If there is a trade show or convention in your city, go to it and ask for the entertainment coordinator and give him or her a promo-package. Then, ask for a business card and follow up with a phone call a few days later.

SUMMARY OF PART II

TO BRANCH OUT YOU WILL NEED:

- Exposure
- Your own unique sound
- The ability to know your audience
- Emotion
- Showmanship and stage presence
- Professionalism with the media
- Good health
- Competition experience that counts
- A tour throughout the US, in other countries with the USO, and on cruise ships

If you have followed the steps to achieving these goals, and have created hype and a strong following, then you are well on your way to relocating to one of the music cities of your choice.

Visit the area first and check out the music venues. Then read the entertainment section of the music city's newspaper, check the classified ads for the real estate and job markets, talk to the local authorities about crime activity in your area of interest, and talk to local residents to get a feel for the area in general.

Return home, where you feel safe and comfortable, review all the information you collected, and determine if this is what you really want.

PART III

RELOCATING AND CAREER BUILDING

CHAPTER 12

♪

MUSIC CITIES

If being a singer is what you must be, if nothing can change your mind and it's in your blood, then it's time to relocate—New York, Los Angeles, Branson, or Nashville. Which music city would be best for you?

Before relocating to any major city, decide the type of music venue you will be basing your career on, and visit that location at least once before moving. You will need a small savings account to act as a cushion, using your income to supplement while you network. Plan to live on that money for at least six months.

To save money, you may have to work an extra parttime job; if you use a coupon at the grocery store, put the savings in the bank; if you get a rebate from a purchase, save it; save your birthday money and Christmas money; make your own birthday, wedding, and Christmas gifts; Take a babysitting job and let someone else do the partying; find other creative ways to save. It may take a while, but giving up a few things now may benefit you later.

NEW YORK

Big Apple: There are many apples
on the success tree, but when you
pick New York City, you pick the
BIG Apple.
...Jazz musicians (1920s-'30s)

New York has five boroughs: Manhattan, the Bronx, Queens, Brooklyn and Staten Island. For those interested in the climate, NYC experiences all four seasons with the average winter temperature ranging between 26 and 42 degrees Fahrenheit. For the temperature on any given day, call (212) 976-1212.

NYC is famous for its Broadway and off-Broadway theatre productions. For more information call (212) 563-2929.

For theater/dance/music performance information, call NYC/On Stage hotline at (212) 768-1818.

Any aspiring singer who wants to sing musicals on or off Broadway should visit these theaters and study the works of others. NYC is famous for its theatre productions and is proud of having some of the best musical talent in the world. Everyone should have the exhilarating experience of attending at least one of the prestigious Broadway theaters.

NYC offers other types of musical opportunities besides musical theatre: gospel, jazz, pop, rap, blues, opera, the symphony orchestra, the NY Philharmonic, R&B, contemporary, country, salsa, and merengue.

New York City is where you will probably want to be if you want to combine acting and singing on stage. Go to a live Broadway performance on your visit to NYC, and pay attention to your level of reaction. If it's what you want to do, save your money and do it.

While in NYC, check out some of the night spots that offer live entertainment. You might consider becoming a singing waitress/waiter at one of them, so that you can earn income while waiting to get discovered.

BROADWAY THEATERS

Walter Kerr Theatre
219 W. 48th Street
New York, NY 10019
(212) 239-6200

Royal Theatre
242 W. 45th Street
New York, NY 10036
(212) 239-6200

Palace Theatre
1564 Broadway
New York, NY 10019
(212) 730-8200

Music Box Theatre
239 W. 45th Street
New York, NY 10036
(212) 239-6200

Winter Garden Theatre
1634 Broadway (50th Street)
New York, NY 10019
(212) 239-6200

Shubert Theatre
225 W. 44th Street
New York, NY 10036
(212) 239-6200

Marquis Theatre
1535 Broadway (46th Street)
New York, NY 10036
(212) 382-0100

Roundabout Theatre Company
1530 Broadway (45th Street)
New York, NY 10036
(212) 869-8400

Eugene O'Neill Theatre
230 W. 49th Street
New York, NY 10036
(212) 239-6200

Martin Beck Theatre
302 W. 45th Street
New York, NY 10036
(212) 239-6200

John Golden Theatre
252 W. 45th Street
New York, NY 10036
(212) 239-6200

Broadhurst Theatre
235 W. 44th Street
New York, NY 10036
(212) 239-6200

Imperial Theatre
249 W. 45 Street
New York, NY 10036
(212) 239-6200

Broadway Theatre
1681 Broadway (53rd Street)
New York, NY 10036
(212) 239-6200

Plymouth Theatre
236 W. 45th Street
New York, NY 10036
(212) 239-6200

Majestic Theater
247 W 44th Street
New York, NY 10036
(212) 239-6200

Gershwin Theater
222 W 51st Street (Broadway)
New York, NY 10019
(212) 586-6510

Minskoff Theater
200 W. 45th Street
New York, NY 10036
(212) 869-0550

St. James Theatre
246 W 44th Street
New York, NY 10036
(212) 239-6200

NIGHTCLUBS

Ambassador Lounge, UN Plaza-Park Hyatt
One UN Plaza
44th Street at 1st Avenue
New York, NY 10017
(212) 702-5014

Bella Napoli
130 Madison Avenue
New York, NY 10016
(212) 683-4510

Cleopatra Supper Club
321 W. 44th Street
New York, NY 10036
(212) 262-1111

Copacabana
617 W. 57th Street
New York, NY 10019
(212) 582-2672

Denim & Diamonds
511 Lexington Avenue
New York, NY 10017
(212) 371-1600

Duplex Cabaret/Piano Bar
61 Christopher Street
New York, NY 10014
(212) 255-5438

Fire House
522 Columbus Avenue
New York, NY 10024
(212) 595-3139

Cotton Club
656 West 125th Street (at Broadway)
New York, NY 10019
(212) 663-7980

Rainbow and Stars (Cabaret)
30 Rockefeller Plaza
New York, NY 10036
(212) 632-5000

Showman's Cafe (jazz club)
375 West 125th Street
New York, NY 10027
(212) 864-8941

There are many other clubs and lounges throughout the NYC area. Clubs and lounges sometime change telephone numbers, street addresses, and names. New ones are added and some close down. A call to the NYC telephone information assistance operator, or checking your telephone business directory at your local college or community library will verify the existence of clubs and lounges before visiting the area.

For additional information on NYC call 800 NYC-visit (800/692-8474), or visit their website: nycvisit.com.

For theatre, dance, music and art in the Bronx write to:

Bronx Council on the Arts
1738 Hone Avenue
Bronx, NY
(718) 931-9500

For information on cultural events in Brooklyn write to:

BACA
200 Eastern Parkway
Brooklyn, New York

For on-going music, dance and readings call the LMCC (Lower Manhattan Cultural Council) at (212) 432-0900.

For cultural events in the Queens call the Queens Council of the Arts at (718) 291-ARTS.

LOS ANGELES

El Pueblo de Nuestra Senora la
Reina de Los Angeles: the town of
the Queen of the Angels.
...Spanish settlers (9/1781)

Los Angeles is a cosmopolitan, international city with a sunny climate and low humidity. The average temperature between November and May is 69 degrees Fahrenheit, and the average temperature between June and October is 80 degrees.

The beautiful Pacific coastline, peaceful deserts, and snow-capped mountains make Los Angeles a desirable place to live while you take advantage of the many entertainment opportunities there.

The city of Los Angeles is comprised of five neighboring regions—Downtown, Hollywood, Westside, Coastal and the Valleys. Los Angeles is famous for its film studios.

Universal Studios-Hollywood
100 Universal City Plaza
Universal City, CA 91608
(818) 508-9600

Paramount Pictures
5555 Melrose Avenue
Hollywood, CA 90038-3197
(213) 956-1777
Warner Bros-The Valleys
4000 Warner Blvd
Burbank, CA 91522
(818) 954-1744

NBC Burbank Studios
3000 W Alameda Avenue STE 1501
Burbank, CA 91523
(818) 840-3537

Because of the desirable climate, musical productions are performed year round, in and out of doors. Los Angeles offers symphonies, opera, chamber music, blues, pop, jazz, country, gospel, reggae, contemporary, salsa, and musicals, either under the open skies, in clubs, coffee houses, or in concert halls. The music city's cultural hub has a trio of musical facilities in downtown Los Angeles—The Dorothy Chandler Pavilion, the Ahmanson, and the Mark Taper Forum, but there are musical productions performed all over the area. Los Angeles is known as being one large stage—talented singers can be heard almost anywhere at any given time.

Los Angeles is where you will want to be if you desire to combine film/television and singing. Visit the area and check out the film studios and some night spots that offer live music. For information on Los Angeles write to:

Los Angeles/convention & Visitors Bureau
685 S Figueroa Street
Los Angeles, CA 90017
(213) 689-8822
(800) CATCH LA

NIGHTCLUBS

Summerfields Lounge
Ramada Beverly Hills
1150 S Beverly Drive
Los Angeles, CA 90035
(310) 553-6561

Westwood Lounge
Westwood Marquis Hotel & Gardens
930 Hilgard Avenue
Los Angeles, CA 90024
(310) 208-8765

Harvelle's Blues Club
1432 Fourth Street
Santa Monica, CA 90401
(310) 395-1676

House of Blues
8430 Sunset Blvd
West Hollywood, CA 90069
(323) 848-5100

The House of Blues offers employment opportunities: After dialing the main number, press "9" for information on jobs at the Los Angeles location; or call the hotline number at (213) 848-4845 for job availability at its other locations. The House of Blues website is: www.hob.com.

There are many other clubs and lounges, where live music is performed, throughout the Los Angeles area. Check the business section of the LA telephone directory at your local library. But keep in mind, clubs and lounges come and go. The few selected for this book are well established.

The LAVCB events hotline is operated 24 hours a day and offers information on current events in English, Japanese, Spanish, French, Italian and German. To call: (213) 689-8822

BRANSON

> Hospitality: It's the people who bring celebrities here to stay. It's a mix of small-town friendliness, Midwestern family values and world-class talent. The residents are committed to hospitality.
>
> ...Dick Hall, Chairman of the Board-Chamber

I include Branson as one of the music cities, because it is a choice location for musicians. Branson's strategy is to bring the fans to the singer, not the other way around. This affords the artist a break from the road.

Branson is growing by leaps and bounds. The Branson/Lakes area includes western Taney county and southern stone county in southwestern Missouri. The city of Branson is located in the Ozark Mountains and is 13 miles north of the Arkansas state line and about 35 miles south of Springfield, Missouri.

Branson has four seasons. The temperature averages from 31 degrees Fahrenheit in January, to 56 degrees in April, to 77 degrees in August, to 35 degrees in December. January and February can bring ice and snow, but the winters are typically mild.

Branson has three dozen indoor theaters, three outdoor theaters and three large theme parks, all with live music shows that total more than sixty different shows with top name entertainers. Artist such as Wayne Newton, Andy Williams, Charley Pride, Tony Orlando, Bobby Vinton and many others perform in Branson; many of the artists have their own theaters. Their music shows include pop, rock'n'roll, country, a variety of bluegrass, western, gospel, jazz and classical music.

Branson's total theater seating capacity is approximately 51,000, exceeding the total seating capacity of the Broadway theaters in NYC. Branson is very proud of that.

If your desire is to perform in one location, then Branson may be for you. Whether you perform in the theatre or night clubs, the fans will come to you. If you really want to relocate to Branson, do it, but follow the same basic guidelines outlined in this book. Travel the club, the fair, and the small concert circuit first. Build a strong following and create hype. Keep sending your schedule to everyone on your mailing list, and when your following comes to Branson to see their favorite stars, they will also come to see you.

Visit Branson and go to one of the music theaters. Get a feel for the type of format the performers use, and get a feel for the level of excitement the performance and atmosphere stirs in you.

Perhaps if you work in one of the clubs, theaters or lounges, you just might get a chance to perform. Build trust.

To subscribe to a magazine that describes Branson activities and gives you information on music events write to:

Branson's Country Review
Circulation Dept
PO Box 357
Branson, MO 65616
(417) 334-6627

Branson Theaters

76 Music Hall
1919 Highway 76W
Branson, MO 65616
(417) 335-2484

Andy Williams' Moon River Theatre
2500 Highway 76W
Branson, MO 65616
(417) 334-4500

Baldknobbers Jamboree Show
2845 Highway 76W PO Box 972
Branson, MO 65616
(417) 334-4528

Bobby Vinton's Blue Velvet Theatre
2701 Highway 76W
Branson, MO 65616
(417) 334-2500

Braschler Music Show
310 Gretna Road
Branson, MO 61656
(417) 334-4363

Campbell's Jubilee
3115 Highway 76W
Branson, MO 61656
(417) 334-6400

Cristy Lane Theatre
3600 Highway 76W PO Box 630
Branson, MO 65616
(417) 335-5111

Crockey's Show Biz Theater
Highway 76W
Branson, MO 65616
(417) 334-4136

Dondino's Theatre
Highway 76W
Branson, MO 65616
(417) 334-4136

Five Star Theatre
Highway 76W
Branson, MO 65616
(417) 334-4136

The Grand Palace
2700 Highway 76W
Branson, MO 65616
(417) 334-7263

Jim Stafford Theatre
3446 Highway 76W
Branson, MO 65616
(417) 335-8080

John Davidson Theatre
High 76W
Branson, MO 65616
(417) 334-4136

Lawrence Welk Champagne Theatre
Highway 76W
Branson, MO 65616
(417) 334-4136

Mel Tillis Theater
PO Box 1626
Branson, MO 65616
(417) 335-8089

Mickey Gilley Theatre
3455 Highway 76W
Branson, MO 65616
(417) 334-3210

Moe Bandy's Americana Theatre
2905 High 76W
Branson, MO 65616
(417) 335-8176

Osmond Family Theater
3216 Highway 76W PO Box 7122
Branson, MO 65616
(417) 336-6100

Owen Theater
Highway 76W
Branson, MO 65616
(417) 334-4136

Ozark Theatre
3800 Highway 76W
Branson, MO 65616
(417) 334-0023

Ozark Theatre 2
Highway 76W
Branson, MO 65616
(417) 334-4136

Presley's Jubilee
2920 Highway 76W
Branson, MO 65616
(417) 334-4874

Pump Boys & Dinettes Theatre
Highway 76W
Branson, MO 65616
(417) 334-4136

Country Tonite Theatre
Highway 76W
Branson, MO 65616
(417) 334-4136

Roy Clark Celebrity Theatre
3431 Highway 76W
Branson, MO 65616
(417) 334-0076

Shoji Tabuchi Theatre
Shepherd of the Hills Expressway
HCRI Box 755
Branson, MO 65616

Thunderbird Theatre
Highway 76W
Branson, MO 65616
(417) 334-4136

Talk of the Town Theatre
(Tony Orlando/Wayne Newton)
464 State Highway 248
Branson, MO 65616
(417) 335-2000

Waltzing Waters
PO Box V
Branson, MO 65616
(417) 334-4144

Shenandoah South Theatre
Highway 76W
Branson, MO 65616
(417) 334-4136

The Will Rogers Theatre
Highway 75W
Branson, MO 65616
(417) 334-4136

Theatres are popular in Branson, but before making a special trip to visit a particular theatre, check with the Chamber of Commerce (listed on page 95) to verify if the artist is still performing there. Most theatres are stable, but depending on artist availability a theatre might change names, or close down.

NIGHTCLUBS

B. T. Bones Steak House
Shepherd of the Hills Expressway
Branson, MO 65616
(417) 335-2002

Beverly's Steak House and Saloon
225 Violyn Drive
Branson, MO 65615
(417) 334-6508

Rocky's Italian Restaurant
120 N. Sycamore Street
Branson, MO 65616
(417) 335-4765

Check the Branson telephone directory at your local library for additional clubs or lounges and their availability. Or check the local telephone directory on your visit to the area.

For additional information on living in Branson write to:

Branson/Lakes Area
Chamber of Commerce
P.O. Box 220
Branson, MO 65615
(417) 334-4136

NASHVILLE

> Although the Nashville metropolitan area is home to more than 1 million people, it is neither so big that you can't find small-town charm, nor so small that you can't find big-city conveniences.
>
> -Nashville Magazine, Chamber of Commerce

Nashville, Tennessee's state capitol, is located in Davidson county. It has been labeled "The Wall Street of the South" for its many financial and insurance firms, "Music City USA" for its entertainment industry, and the "Athens of the South" for its many prestigious colleges, universities, and technical schools.

Nashville is proud of the Grand Ole Opry, but is equally proud of its Nashville Symphony, ballet, opera, and Tennessee Repertory Theatre.

Nashville has a moderate climate with an average annual temperature of 59.2 degrees Fahrenheit. Averages for January are 46.3 degrees to 27.8 degrees. The temperatures in June range from 89.8 degrees to 69.0 degrees. The average annual precipitation is 48.49 inches, and the average humidity is 58 percent.

Nashville offers a variety of music opportunities. There are musical performances—opera, ballet and the symphony—at the Tennessee Performing Arts Center. There is blues music, as well as alternative rock and country at area night clubs and lounges.

The city's night clubs showcases the best of the local singers, songwriters and musicians. There is gospel, bluegrass, and hip hop at various venues around Nashville, but because it is known as the home of country music, I will put the emphasis on that.

The Grand Ole Opry is the home of many great country artists. It is an honor for a country artist to be accepted into the Grand Ole Opry, and for them to perform on the prestigious stage. Each year the Opry hosts the CMA awards show.

The Ryman Auditorium, which was the home of the Opry from 1943 to 1974, has been restored, and live music performances can once again be seen and heard on stage. Outdoor festivals and concerts are held at the Riverfront Park located near the Cumberland River at the end of town.

More than 1,500 companies and 25,000 people are involved in the music entertainment industry in Nashville. There are approximately 68 record labels, 195 recording studios, 130 music publishing companies, 189 booking agents, 10 record manufacturers, and 33 record promotion companies. Nashville's music publishing industry is driven by songwriting, which is the foundation of the Nashville music industry.

MAJOR RECORD LABELS

Asylum Records
1906 Acklen Avenue
Nashville, TN 37203
(615) 292-7990

Arista Records
7 Music Circle N
Nashville, TN 37203
(615) 780-9100

Atlantic Records
1812 Broadway
Nashville, TN 37203
(615) 327-9394

Benson Records
365 Great Circle Drive
Nashville, TN 37228
(615) 742-6800

BNA Entertainment
call for appointment
(615) 780-4400

.Curb Records
47 Music Square E
Nashville, TN 37203
(615) 321-5080

Giant Records
1514 South Street
Nashville, TN 37212
(616) 256-3110

Liberty Records
3322 West End Ave
11th floor
Nashville, TN 37206
(615) 269-2000

MCA Records
60 Music Square E
Nashville, TN 37203
(615) 244-8944

Mercury Nashville
66 Music Square W
Nashville, TN 37203
(615) 320-0110

RCA Records
1 Music Circle N
Nashville, TN 37203
(615) 664-1200

Reunion Records
2910 Poston Avenue
Nashville, TN 37203
(615) 320-9200

Sony Music
34 Music Square E
Nashville, TN 37203
(615) 742-4321

Warner/Reprise Nashville
20 Music Square E
Nashville, TN 37203
(615) 748-8000

Word, Inc.
3319 West End Avenue #200
Nashville, TN 37206
(615) 385-9673

NASHVILLE'S LARGEST PUBLISHING COMPANIES

ALMO/Irving Music Publishing
1904 Adelicia
Nashville, TN 37212
(615) 321-0820

BMG Music Publishing
1 Music Circle N
Nashville, TN 37203
(615) 780-5420

EMI Music Publishing
35 Music Square E
Nashville, TN 37203
(615) 742-8081

MCA Music Publishing
1114 17th Avenue S
Nashville, TN 37208
(615) 327-4622

Opryland Music Group
65 Music Square W
Nashville, TN 37203
(615) 321-5550

Polygram/Island Music Publishing Group
54 Music Square E Suite 200
Nashville, TN 37203
(615) 256-7648

Sony/Tree
Tree Publishing Co., Inc.
Cross Keys Publishing Co., Inc.
1111 16th Avenue S
Nashville, TN 37208
(615) 726-0890

Warner/Chappell Music, Inc.
21 Music Square E
Nashville, TN 37203
(615) 254-8777

Word Music Group
33 Music Square W
Nashville, TN 37203
(615) 385-9653

NIGHTCLUBS

Tootsie's Orchid Lounge
422 Broadway
Nashville, TN 37203
(615) 726-3739

Wildhorse Saloon
116 Second Avenue N
Nashville, TN 37201
(615) 256-9453

The Stockyard Restaurant
(Country music-upstairs)
Manhatten's Dinner Club
(Big Band music-downstairs)
901 Second Avenue N
Nashville, TN 37201
(615) 255-6464

The Station Inn
402 12th Avenue S
Nashville, TN 37208
(615) 255-3307

Bell Cove Club
141 Sunset Drive
Hendersonville, TN 37207
(615) 822-7074

Holiday Inn Vanderbilt's
Commodore Lounge
2613 West End Avenue
Nashville, TN 37206
(615) 327-4707

Douglas Corner Cafe
2106A Eight Ave S
Nashville, TN 37204
(615) 298-1688

The Exit/In
2208 Elliston Place
Nashville, TN 37203
(615) 321-4400

The Sutler
2608 Franklin Road
Nashville, TN 37204
(615) 297-9195

Bluebird Cafe
4104 Hillsboro Road
Nashville, TN 37215
(615) 383-1461

Nashville Palace
2400 Music Valley Drive
Nashville, TN 37214
(615) 885-1540

Gaylord Opryland Hotel and Resort Center
2800 Opryland Drive
Nashville, TN 37214
(615) 889-1000

3rd & Lindsey Bar and Grill
818 Third Avenue S
Nashville, TN 37210
(615) 259-1597

The Pub of Love
123 12th Avenue N
Nashville, TN 37203
(615) 256-5683

12th & Porter Playroom
114 12th Avenue N
Nashville, TN 37203
(615) 254-7236

328 Performance Hall
328 Fourth Avenue S
Nashville, TN 37219
(615) 259-3288

Hard Rock Cafe
Second Avenue
Nashville, TN 37201
(615) 742-9900

For a listing of recording studios, agents, managers, recording manufacturers, record promotion companies, publicity companies and other music industry companies, write to:

Music Business Directory
PO Box 120675
Nashville, TN 37212
(615) 255-1068

There are too many companies to list here, but you can find them in the business section of a Nashville telephone directory, in the Music Business Directory, or by becoming a member of the Country Music Association (CMA). Being a member of the CMA gives you voting privileges for the Country Music Award nominations, access to information on managers, artists, agents, and a listing of radio stations across the United States. As a member, you also receive a subscription to <u>Close</u> <u>Up</u>, a monthly magazine that keeps you abreast of your favorite stars and music industry information. To become a member write to:

The Country Music Association
One Music Circle South
Nashville, TN 37203
(615) 244-2840
Or browse the CMA website at: www.country music.org.

OTHER NASHVILLE MUSIC EVENTS

Annually, in mid-June, fans from around the world gather in Nashville for the International Country Music Fan Fair for a full week of festivities. Fan Fair was established for the fans by the recording artists, as a way to thank them for their loyalty and devotion. There is an admission fee which entitles you to attend over 30 hours of spectacular stage shows, a bluegrass concert, the Grand Masters Fiddling Championship, picture and autograph sessions, two lunches, tickets for the Country Music Hall of Fame, Opryland USA, and the Ryman Auditorium. (Children age three and under are admitted free.) Fan Fair is held at the Tennessee State Fairgrounds and offers free parking. For tickets write to:

Fan Fair
2804 Opryland Drive
Nashville, TN 37214
(615) 889-7503

At midnight on Saturday nights, the Ernest Tubb Record Shop holds a live radio show which features Opry stars and new talent. The Ernest Tubb Record Shop Midnight Jamboree is held at:

Ernest Tubb Record Shop
2414 Music Valley Drive
Nashville, TN 37214
(615) 889-2474

The Ernest Tubb Record Shop website is: www.etrs.net

If you are interested in seeing a live, free TV taping of your favorite Nashville network country music show, call Prime Time Country at (615) 889-6611.

There is a concert venue for country and bluegrass music at 116 Fifth Avenue North, Nashville, TN 37219. Phone number: (615) 254-1445.

The Martha White-Lester Flatt Hometown Memorial Festival for amateurs and professionals alike is in June. Write to:

Martha White-Lester Flatt Memorial Festival
Route 5, Box 509
Sparta, Tennessee 38583
Or call the White County Chamber of Commerce at (931) 836-3552.

For additional information on living in Nashville write to:

Nashville Area Chamber of Commerce
161 Fourth Avenue North
Nashville, TN 37219
(615) 259-4755
Or call the Nashville Visitors Center at (615) 259-4700.
www.MUSICCITYUSA.CitySearch.com

 **NOTES** 

CHAPTER 13

NETWORKING

Once you have selected the music city of your choice, arrived at your music city destination, opened up a checking account, and moved into your new apartment or rooming house, it is time to take action. Now that you are where you want to be, you have to start the chain of events that will lead to stardom. No one is going to hunt you down. Nothing is going to happen unless you make it happen.

Your next step on the climb to career building is to meet the right people. Start networking immediately.

First, get a job. Work in a restaurant where the industry people hang out, close to studios and music offices. Take any job where you will meet people in the business and have some kind of income. Try music stores, record shops, electronics stores, or any of the record companies, management offices and agencies of any type. An excellent way to start working immediately, sometimes the same day, is through one of the temporary services listed in the 'phone book under "Temporaries", "Manpower," "AES," or any other agency to which you don't have to pay a fee. The pay isn't great, but it's income. Tell them you would like a position in the music industry if one becomes available. If you have a particular skill—typing, computer knowledge, sales, accounting, or writing ability—the chances are even better. Remember, everyone you meet is related to someone else, and that someone else may be in the music business.

Now that you have an apartment and are working, the easiest way to meet music business professionals and other aspiring music industry people, is to attend seminars, hang out where they hang out, and if possible, sign up for a college course. You never know which of the other students will end up giving you that needed break sometime in the future. Most seminars and classes are taught by someone in the industry, especially the night college courses.

An excellent course for you to start with is a music business course. You will learn how to work with agents, managers, contracts, attorneys; in other words, you'll learn the total process. More than likely the instructor has a network of music business people and entertainment attorneys. Now someone associated with the business knows you by name and sight. Make an impression. Listen and learn. If money is tight, take one course at a time, and learn your lessons well.

Another effective networking technique, if you can afford it, is to sign up with a private vocal coach. Ask your music business instructor to recommend someone for you. Not only will you be working with another person with contacts, but the vocal coach can help develop your voice and your particular style. Usually the vocal coach has several students and will give recitals for their families and friends; you never know who might show up. You can get bad advice all day and learn by trial and error on your own, or you can go about it more easily and attain your goals much more quickly by networking and listening to the experts.

Don't demand or ask for unreasonable favors. If you really have the talent, are able to develop a unique sound that belongs only to you, and are willing to work hard in the right direction, people will want to help you. If you have all the answers, are a know-it-all, and give the impression that you don't need advice from the right people, stay home. Professionals don't have time to raise you.

When you do meet the music business people, try to meet them on their turf—the seminars, conventions, showcases—not necessarily at parties where they may drink a little too much and won't even remember you the next day. Not all music business people drink, or drink excessively, but be selective about parties. The major artists are too busy keeping their own careers going, so hanging out at parties they attend probably won't get you very far. But if you are lucky enough to get invited to a private function at a major artist's house, go if you have the time. You might learn some road tips or behind-the-scene activity, or what not to do through their experiences. Rather than hanging out with the major artists, concentrate on meeting different people through other methods, such as musicians, studio engineers, or other performers on your level. They all know people, too. Network about 50 percent of your spare time and work on your art the other 50 percent. Don't burn yourself out to the point it has a negative impact on you or your performance. If you keep in mind that failures are only stepping stones to success, then you will ultimately succeed. If you take the right steps, really have talent, are a team player, and have the tenacity to stick to your goals, you'll eventually get noticed and it will be well worth the wait. Alan Jackson worked and hung out in Nashville for several years. He wouldn't give up, kept a positive attitude, had a friendly smile for all, and worked at it until someone noticed. Look at Alan today. Alan is putting out hit songs, receiving awards for his efforts, and is signed by Arista Records, a top independent recording company in Nashville. Madonna, on the other side of the coin, hung out in New York City, determined to be noticed by the world. She believed in herself even if others didn't. Her belief, and her tenacity was so strong that she did make herself known to the world. She went on to win a Golden Globe Award for her outstanding performance in the Golden Globe Award winning movie—"Evita."

Alan and Madonna each had the desire to succeed; each took different career directions, but both proved it could be done at the level they strived for. They wouldn't give up. They dedicated themselves to succeed, and they did. Alan went the "normal" route, while Madonna at times was somewhat unconventional. The point being, they each ended up at a level of success they feel comfortable with. Alan is as successful in his own right as Modonna is in hers. You determine your own level of success. You have the opportunity to go as far as you are willing to sacrifice. So, If you have a strong desire to succeed, and take the necessary action, you too can achieve your level of success.

 **NOTES** 

CHAPTER 14

THE BUSINESS PROFESSIONALS

It is time to pitch yourself to an agent or manager when you have something to offer, know how to offer it, and have the intelligence to know when to offer it. Timing, as they say in the theatre, is everything. So prepare yourself properly in order to talk to the professionals, if and when the opportunity presents itself. Most of the time you will take the initiative to schedule meetings, but sometimes you may meet just the right person at just the right gathering.

You do not have to know every detail about the music business, but you should at least know why you are hiring the professionals. You should know what they will do for you, and you should keep up with the industry trends. Be well informed.

Your personal representatives, agents, and managers have two distinct responsibilities, and both are important to your career. The agent finds you work and negotiates the terms and conditions of your contract; the business manager handles your career development, gives you personal business advice and moral support, and plans your future career strategy.

Agents are listed in the business section of the telephone directory and in other music business directories. In the country field, check the music business directory. Also check with the Country Music Association and venues that book artists. Once you compile a list, check with the Better Business Bureau for references on the agencies you've never heard of. Call the reputable agencies and ask if they are receiving new artist material. Managers are listed in the same source directories in which agents are found, and are also listed on the backs of cassettes, Cds, and videos.

AGENTS

You will probably want to hire an agent first. You will need the steady work and media hype before signing on with a manager. Agents should work extremely hard at keeping your calendar full. For this they get ten to fifteen percent of your gross salary. Unless you are dealing with a major agency, you might not want to sign an exclusive contract. If possible, let several agencies find you work until you decide which agency is best for you. An agent usually handles a number of artists at the same time (a stable of talent) and works closely with your manager.

Booking agents not only work with managers, they also work with promoters. Promoters buy the talent from the booking agent and together they plan performance dates, any commitments or special requests from either party, sign contracts, and determine how the singer will be advertised at that particular venue. The agency will usually supply a large poster of the artist, pictures for publicity, and any material to aid in radio and television promotion. The promoter is responsible for the advertising and promotional costs. He also pays the performing artist according to the terms and agreements written in the contract, and the agency's job is to ensure that this will happen.

MANAGERS

When you do find a manager, have an entertainment attorney review the Artist/Management contract before signing. An artist does not want to be bound for life with the same manager, if that manager isn't doing a good job. Nor does a good manager want to be bound to an artist that isn't performing. The manager may not ask you to sign a contract until he sees how you work together, but a signed contract prevents potential problems down the road.

You will usually sign an exclusive contract for one or two years, with yearly options of up to five years. Your entertainment attorney will create an artist/management contract according to the terms and conditions you and your manager agree on. Some artists change managers as their career outgrows the manager's capabilities, while other artists keep the same manager throughout their entire careers. It's a judgment call.

The business manager plays many roles but does not handle the artist's money. The artist or an accountant does that. The business manager oversees all business aspects of the artist's career. For this, the manager usually receives between 10 to 35 percent of the artist's gross earnings, plus expenses for travel if you request their presence on the road. A different person—the road manager—usually travels on the road with the artist and handles money transactions and takes care of problems that arise at the venues.

Business managers deal with agents, promoters, record companies, public relation firms, publishers, production companies, and sometimes accountants, attorneys, financial investors, and anyone else connected to the business end of the artist's career. They also often become a personal confidante to the artist and helps to keep the artist focused on his or her career path.

Unlike the agent, the manager handles a small number of artists. Artists and their careers require a lot of dedicated time. A manager that handles too many artists cannot be completely effective. You do not need a manager with a fancy office or big names on his or her roster. All you need is an manager that can make things happen and one who has the right contacts.

When you reach major star status, you'll often be able to re-negotiate your artist/management contract to a smaller percentage rate, or sometimes to a percentage rate based on net earnings, rather than net gross. There are many options and this is where an entertainment attorney is extremely helpful.

ENTERTAINMENT ATTORNEYS

The role of the entertainment attorney has increased in importance over the past couple of decades. The entertainment attorney usually has powerful connections, has built a solid reputation, and has the experience to advise the recording artist and songwriter in business, as well as in legal matters.

Contracts can be written to best represent the other party, leaving the artist in a sticky situation when a problem arises. It is important to have an entertainment attorney review all legal documents before you sign them.

Entertainment attorneys can be very helpful with contracts or money matters, and sometimes can set you up with meeting the right people. They are powerful influences, and if you possess that most desirable trait—a rare talent, an entertainment attorney can open doors that otherwise might be closed forever. Because the entertainment attorney has good contacts in the music business he or she just might get your tape or video to an agent, record company, or manager. Mary Chapin-Carpenter was introduced to Nashville through an entertainment attorney. If you are a songwriter, and the song has merit, the entertainment attorney might be the one that gets it to a publisher.

Attorneys, in general, can be costly, but an entertainment attorney could be a investment worth looking into. Many entertainment attorneys charge an hourly rate, plus a retainer fee. The hourly rate usually runs between $150 to $450, with extra billing for items that could include telephone calls, court filing fees, overnight mailings and fax charges. There may be other charges, as well.

A retainer is an overall monthly (or yearly) fee between an attorney and a client who have continuing legal business, and for which the attorney will be consistently available to the client. The client will pay a set fee each month, and the attorney will deduct business expenses from that fee.

Sometimes the entertainment attorney will charge a flat fee, one cost for the entire project. Some also charge a percentage of the client's earnings above the hourly or flat fee. For example, if you receive a $100,000 signing advance for a record deal, the attorney could either be entitled to a one-time percentage of the initial $100,000, or if the artist receives additional advances, could be entitled to a percentage for a specified period of time. Before hiring an entertainment attorney, make sure you clearly understand all the financial data and rate agreements.

You will need an entertainment attorney eventually, for legal music business contracts, so it would be a good idea to talk to one early in your career and gain some insight into the business. Ask your friends in the business which attorneys they're using.

Because entertainment attorneys are powerful sources, they are also very busy. Before approaching one with a promo-package or song, be prepared and present yourself professionally.

ACCOUNTANTS

One other professional who would be an asset when you are ready is the accountant. He will keep your financial affairs in-tact while you are traveling. If you hire an accountant, make sure to check your account quarterly, and review all documents before signing. Choose an accountant with an established reputation; ask the professionals for recommendations and check with the Better Business Bureau.

If an accountant prepares your income taxes, always review each line item thoroughly. If you don't understand any part of the prepared taxes, then ask questions until you are completely satisfied with the answer.

TAXES AND THE IRS

You are now a business and you will have to pay taxes. Keep all business receipts, including meals and lodging and other travel expenses. Keep a log of miles travelled, times, dates, venue, and contact name. Keep a record of any monies you make and spend.

The Internal Revenue Service allows you to deduct a portion of your house—heat, electricity, insurance, phone calls, rent or mortgage—if that portion is used on an exclusive and regular basis as your principal place of business. If this portion of your house is used for exclusive and regular extensive rehearsals, coaching, or practicing of any kind pertaining to your career, then it is tax deductible.

When you start making a sizeable income as a performing artist, you will want to seek the advice of a music business accountant or an entertainment attorney on such items as low income performing, artist's special deduction allowance, shifting taxable income to persons in lower tax brackets, shifting income from one year to another based on a fiscal or calendar year, Keogh plans, individual retirement accounts (IRAs), incorporating, and any other tax items that change from time to time.

A very important lesson to learn from Willie Nelson, Dottie West, and Redd Fox is to never leave your tax matters in the hands of others. You are solely responsible for your own income tax return. Always check it thoroughly before signing. Willie, Dottie, and Redd lost everything they owned when the IRS confiscated their assets (including personal family albums). They depended on others to do right by them. So, know your own business. If someone else prepares your taxes, make sure that you understand each line item before signing the IRS form, which is a legal document. Don't be the IRS's next victim; no one else but you will pay.

If an error does occur, and the IRS sends you a notice, take care of the problem immediately. Every day the problem exists, interest and penalties will be added to the amount owed. These can quickly exceed the original amount. This is one area in which to be educated. Seek advice, take a course in taxes, and don't hire an accountant that doesn't understand the music business.

FINANCIAL BACKER

A financial backer is a person who believes in your talent and is willing to invest money in you. He will agree to finance your professional demo audio tape, video tape, and/or CD for a percentage of sales, once you have achieved success. If you are lucky enough to find such a person, then you may have an easier time finding a manager.

To find an investor, it's best to have your entertainment attorney already on board, or an accountant that understands the music business, and ask him to advise you on putting together a presentable proposal. Usually the entertainment attorney, or music business accountant, will know what items you will need for an artist proposal to be presented to an investor. After the proposal is complete, write a solid cover letter to the person you have in mind, and state why you feel that investor will receive a return on his investment.

The person you choose as a financial backer is usually one who knows you and your talent, and feels that you will be a good financial risk. By the same token, it's important for you to know the credibility of the backer before signing any agreements with him or her.

If you find a reputable investor, and he or she likes your proposal, seek the aid of an attorney. Be careful not to get hooked for life. Your dealings with financial backers should be for the particular items they are investing in, and not your future recordings or other forms of entertainment.

If you can't afford an entertainment attorney, check around for prices on recording and video productions, and put together the best financial package you can. Write a strong, sincere cover letter.

The first page in the proposal will include your name, address and telephone number, as well as the type of music career for which you are seeking financing. Then state the purpose of the proposal, i.e. "For your review as a potential financial investor for all, or any part of the funds needed to back (your name) in a musical career."

The next page would state your proposal contents: production schedule, budget summary, anticipated questions/answers for investors, your qualifications (bio sheet), a sample of your present performance schedule, an 8 X 10 picture, and a note stating that a demo tape is included.

The pages that follow will be a breakdown of the summary sheet. You will need to know the costs of producing a recording and a music video, the costs of mass duplication, promotion and publicity, and the costs of any important conventions and showcases at which you will be performing.

The financial investor will want to know how soon the project will return his investment, how much of a return can be expected, and what markets there are for the album, single records, Cds, and videos. Although an artist cannot categorically state or guarantee these things he should have a realistic plan. The music business is a gamble, true, but is a business just the same. All start-up businesses require a business plan.

For the latter question, list the various markets of distribution—personal appearances, television, radio, publications, foreign, conventions, showcases, fan clubs, and other types of entertainment (film or stage). Financial backers want to know who your audience will be; the country music fans, cross-over blues, gospel, rock/roll or a combination, as well as who your agent and manager are. He will want to know if your business manager has a reputable business track record, why you feel you and your manager will be able to accomplish the goals set forth in the proposal, and if the business manager has the necessary skills to manage all stages of the project.

If financial backers wants to participate in the project, tell them that you will keep them updated on all financial activities pertaining to the agreed project, that they will be invited to special events (when feasible), that they will receive a copy of the album, and that you (the artist), will take personal responsibility to see that they reap financial rewards on their investment. (Which is YOU.) The financial backer is an investor, and unless he or she is involved in the music business already, it is best to keep personal and business dealings separate.

Don't forget to include your best demo tape in your investors proposal package, as you hope your investor will finance your professional demo tape/CD to hand out to managers, agents, and others.

 **NOTES** 

CHAPTER 15

PROFESSIONALISM AND ORIGINALITY OF SOUND AND SONG

PROFESSIONAL DEMO

There are two types of professional studio recordings: a master recording and a demonstration recording.

The master is the top of the line quality recording and is usually much more expensive. It is a commercially marketable recording and is ready for mass distribution.

The demonstration (demo) is a quality recording which is used for the sole purpose of marketing the artist or songwriter's talent to music business professionals; it is not for immediate monetary gain.

The professional demo recording is what you will put in your promotional package to aid in securing an agent, manager and, eventually, a recording contract. The demo recording costs less than a master because you do not sell this product. If you want to record a tape or CD to sell at concerts, then you will need a master recording and will pay union musician scale.

It is as important to pick a good studio and sound engineer for a demo recording as it is for a master recording. The quality of sound is essential for both. Your sound is you, so make it the best you can afford.

In Nashville, a typical recording session usually will require seven instrumentalists and one to four backup singers. It all depends on the sound you are going for and who you are pitching to. If you are pitching songs to a publisher, a simple demo is all that is necessary, and a session should take around three hours and cost around $2000. If you are pitching to a record company you might want to consider a master quality tape because you will want to project the best audio product of your singing voice. A quality master tape may attract experienced union musicians—musicians who play for major artists and are on break from the road. Contact the Musician's Union at (615) 244-9514.

For a master session, the musician will earn full union scale, twice the cost of a regular demo session. A master session may take a little longer to produce because quality is a must, and will probably cost around $4000; more for extras—added strings, special sound effects, etc. (The more established the producer, the more the costs increase). Another advantage of choosing to produce a master quality versus a regular demo is that if a particular song shows promise and arouses interest, it can be reproduced without having to pay additional costs. If you produce a regular demo and a particular song is exceptional, according to the musician's union, you will have to pay full union scale to upgrade that song.

When deciding whether to produce a less expensive regular demo, or the more expensive master quality demo, consider your purpose for the tape and any plans you have for particular songs. If you feel you will be "picked-up" by a record company, by all means, pay for a good "demo" tape. If the record company "picks-you-up", they will pay for a master recording.

Once you have decided on the type of demo, you will need to schedule the recording studio, the sound engineer, producer, and musicians. Most studios have their own sound engineer and producer already, but if you have a preference you can usually hire your own. Studios can cost from $250 to $500 a session, and the sound engineer's earnings are often figured into that price. If you shop around you may be able to rent a studio for less. Check the musician's union for musicians and contact them for availability. Also, check with the sound engineer. He or she might know some musicians who are temporarily off the road, and perhaps could put you in touch with a reputable moonlighting producer. Before going into the studio, have your songs down pat and make copies of the lyric sheets for everyone involved. Start the session off with two upbeat songs with catchy hooks, followed by a solid ballad. If your ballad is your best representation, then you would start with it. The idea is to make the listeners want to hear more and give them something they have never heard—all originals.

"Original" is the key word here. Keep your style consistent so that it identifies you. No matter what the song, let it be you singing it with your unique voice. Hire backup singers for effect; don't try to do it all.

ORIGINAL SONGS

Original songs can come from a wide variety of sources. Publishers may give you some songs the major artists have turned down. These probably are not great, but there could be a good song that has been overlooked by everyone else; if you recognize its potential, it's yours. Another way to find songs is to ask some of the songwriters you have met if they have any songs for you to consider. If not, ask if they know of someone who does. Also ask your music business instructor and ask your vocal coach, or try writing some songs of your own. If you think you have the talent, take a music writing course. If you do write your own songs, you will want to copyright them and will want to join Broadcast Music, Inc. (BMI) or American Society of Composers, Authors, and Publishers (ASCAP).

SONG WRITING

> Contrary to popular misconception,
> songwriting is not an inspiration
> business. It is a craft: technique
> supporting talent.
>
> Sheila Davis

Songwriters first determine whether they have talent, then work on developing that talent by the use of proven techniques. To be a successful songwriter you will have to follow a logical order of sequence:

* Start with an idea the masses can identify with
* Assign an unforgettable title
* Grab the listeners' attention (the who & what)
* Have a strong hook to keep their attention
* Spark an emotional response
* Organize the song structure so that it makes sense

Many writers get their ideas from personal experiences. Some ideas make great songs, while others do not. Whether or not it makes a good song depends on the writer's ability to take a personal experience, remove the personal, and turn it into a general experience. Once the experience becomes general, the writer then needs to find some situations to visualize that general experience to make it personal again. Take the song "Crazy", recorded by Patsy Cline and written by Willie Nelson: Willie wrote about being crazy for feeling lonely and blue, probably over a jilted lover—personal experience. Because a good number of people have felt lonely and blue at sometime in their lives, they can relate to the song—the general listening audience. The song goes on to situations where the writer speaks of feeling "crazy for hurting", "crazy for crying", and "crazy for loving you". Individuals, listening to the song can visualize their own sad situations and feel their own emotional pain—becomes personal to them. If songwriters use the Personal-General-Personal theory, ideas become songs for the masses, songs that most individuals can relate to in one way or another, songs in which the singer can identify with the story and feel the emotional impact. The singer will then be able to express that emotion to individual listeners in such a way that the listener can give an emotional response. When the writer, the singer, and the listener relate and respond to the heart of a song as though the song were meant for them alone—their personal story—the song becomes a hit. This is good song writing.

Application Form PA

Detach and read these instructions before completing this form. Make sure all applicable spaces have been filled in before you return this form.

When to Use This Form: Use Form PA for registration of published or unpublished works of the performing arts. This class includes works prepared for the purpose of being "performed" directly before an audience or indirectly "by means of any device or process." Works of the performing arts include: (1) musical works, including any accompanying words; (2) dramatic works, including any accompanying music; (3) pantomimes and choreographic works; and (4) motion pictures and other audiovisual works.

Deposit to Accompany Application: An application for copyright registration must be accompanied by a deposit consisting of copies or phonorecords representing the entire work for which registration is made. The following are the general deposit requirements as set forth in the statute:

Unpublished Work: Deposit one complete copy (or phonorecord).

Published Work: Deposit two complete copies (or one phonorecord) of the best edition.

Work First Published Outside the United States: Deposit one complete copy (or phonorecord) of the first foreign edition.

Contribution to a Collective Work: Deposit one complete copy (or phonorecord) of the best edition of the collective work.

Motion Pictures: Deposit *both* of the following: (1) a separate written description of the contents of the motion picture; and (2) for a published work, one complete copy of the best edition of the motion picture; or, for an unpublished work, one complete copy of the motion picture or identifying material. Identifying material may be either an audiorecording of the entire soundtrack or one frame enlargement or similar visual print from each 10-minute segment.

The Copyright Notice: Before March 1, 1989, the use of copyright notice was mandatory on all published works, and any work first published before that date should have carried a notice. For works first published on and after March 1, 1989, use of the copyright notice is optional. For more information about copyright notice, see Circular 3, "Copyright Notice."

For Further Information: To speak to an information specialist, call (202) 707-3000 (TTY: (202) 707-6737). Recorded information is available 24 hours a day. Order forms and other publications from the address in space 9 or call the Forms and Publications Hotline at (202) 707-9100. Most circulars (but not forms) are available via fax. Call (202) 707-2600 from a touchtone phone. Access and download circulars, forms, and other information from the Copyright Office Website at http://www.loc.gov/copyright.

PRIVACY ACT ADVISORY STATEMENT Required by the Privacy Act of 1974 (P.L. 93-579)

The authority for requesting this information is title 17, U.S.C., secs. 409 and 410. Furnishing the requested information is voluntary. But if the information is not furnished, it may be necessary to delay or refuse registration and you may not be entitled to certain relief, remedies, and benefits provided in chapters 4 and 5 of title 17, U.S.C.

The principal uses of the requested information are the establishment and maintenance of a public record and the examination of the application for compliance with the registration requirements of the copyright code.

Other routine uses include public inspection and copying, preparation of public indexes, preparation of public catalogs of copyright registrations, and preparation of search reports upon request.

NOTE: No other advisory statement will be given in connection with this application. Please keep this statement and refer to it if we communicate with you regarding this application.

Please type or print using black ink. The form is used to produce the certificate.

1 SPACE 1: Title

Title of This Work: Every work submitted for copyright registration must be given a title to identify that particular work. If the copies or phonorecords of the work bear a title (or an identifying phrase that could serve as a title), transcribe that wording *completely* and *exactly* on the application. Indexing of the registration and future identification of the work will depend on the information you give here. If the work you are registering is an entire "collective work" (such as a collection of plays or songs), give the overall title of the collection. If you are registering one or more individual contributions to a collective work, give the title of each contribution, followed by the title of the collection. For an unpublished collection, you may give the titles of the individual works after the collection title.

Previous or Alternative Titles: Complete this space if there are any additional titles for the work under which someone searching for the registration might be likely to look, or under which a document pertaining to the work might be recorded.

Nature of This Work: Briefly describe the general nature or character of the work being registered for copyright. Examples: "Music"; "Song Lyrics"; "Words and Music"; "Drama"; "Musical Play"; "Choreography"; "Pantomime"; "Motion Picture"; "Audiovisual Work."

SPACE 2: Author(s)

General Instructions: After reading these instructions, decide who are the "authors" of this work for copyright purposes. Then, unless the work is a "collective work," give the requested information about every "author" who contributed any appreciable amount of copyrightable matter to this version of the work. If you need further space, request additional Continuation Sheets. In the case of a collective work, such as a songbook or a collection of plays, give the information about the author of the collective work as a whole.

Name of Author: The fullest form of the author's name should be given. Unless the work was "made for hire," the individual who actually created the work is its "author." In the case of a work made for hire, the statute provides that "the employer or other person for whom the work was prepared is considered the author."

What is a "Work Made for Hire"? A "work made for hire" is defined as: (1) "a work prepared by an employee within the scope of his or her employment"; or (2) "a work specially ordered or commissioned for use as a contribution to a collective work, as a part of a motion picture or other audiovisual work, as a translation, as a supplementary work, as a compilation, as an instructional text, as a test, as answer material for a test, or as an atlas, if the parties expressly agree in a written instrument signed by them that the work shall be considered a work made for hire." If you have checked "Yes" to indicate that the work was "made for hire," you must give the full legal name of the employer (or other person for whom the work was prepared). You may also include the name of the employee along with the name of the employer (for example: "Elster Music Co., employer for hire of John Ferguson").

"Anonymous" or "Pseudonymous" Work: An author's contribution to a work is "anonymous" if that author is not identified on the copies or phonorecords of the work. An author's contribution to a work is "pseudonymous" if that author is identified on the copies or phonorecords under a fictitious name. If the work is "anonymous" you may: (1) leave the line blank; or (2) state "anonymous" on the line; or (3) reveal the author's identity. If the work is "pseudonymous" you may: (1) leave the line blank; or (2) give the pseudonym and identify it as such (example: "Huntley Haverstock, pseudonym"); or (3) reveal the author's name, making clear which is the real name and which is the pseudonym (for example: "Judith Barton, whose pseudonym is Madeline Elster"). However, the citizenship or domicile of the author **must** be given in all cases.

Dates of Birth and Death: If the author is dead, the statute requires that the year of death be included in the application unless the work is anonymous or pseudonymous. The author's birth date is optional, but is useful as a form of identification. Leave this space blank if the author's contribution was a "work made for hire."

Author's Nationality or Domicile: Give the country of which the author is a citizen, or the country in which the author is domiciled. Nationality or domicile **must** be given in all cases.

Nature of Authorship: Give a brief general statement of the nature of this particular author's contribution to the work. Examples: "Words"; "Coauthor of Music"; "Words and Music"; "Arrangement"; "Coauthor of Book and Lyrics"; "Dramatization"; "Screen Play"; "Compilation and English Translation"; "Editorial Revisions."

*Registration filing fees are effective through June 30, 1999. After that date, please write the Copyright Office, check the Copyright Office Website at http://www.loc.gov/copyright, or call (202) 707-3000 for the latest fee information.

3 SPACE 3: Creation and Publication

General Instructions: Do not confuse "creation" with "publication." Every application for copyright registration must state "the year in which creation of the work was completed." Give the date and nation of first publication only if the work has been published.

Creation: Under the statute, a work is "created" when it is fixed in a copy or phonorecord for the first time. Where a work has been prepared over a period of time, the part of the work existing in fixed form on a particular date constitutes the created work on that date. The date you give here should be the year in which the author completed the particular version for which registration is now being sought, even if other versions exist or if further changes or additions are planned.

Publication: The statute defines "publication" as "the distribution of copies or phonorecords of a work to the public by sale or other transfer of ownership, or by rental, lease, or lending"; a work is also "published" if there has been an "offering to distribute copies or phonorecords to a group of persons for purposes of further distribution, public performance, or public display." Give the full date (month, day, year) when, and the country where, publication first occurred. If first publication took place simultaneously in the United States and other countries, it is sufficient to state "U.S.A."

4 SPACE 4: Claimant(s)

Name(s) and Address(es) of Copyright Claimant(s): Give the name(s) and address(es) of the copyright claimant(s) in this work even if the claimant is the same as the author. Copyright in a work belongs initially to the author of the work (including, in the case of a work made for hire, the employer or other person for whom the work was prepared). The copyright claimant is either the author of the work or a person or organization to whom the copyright initially belonging to the author has been transferred.

Transfer: The statute provides that, if the copyright claimant is not the author, the application for registration must contain "a brief statement of how the claimant obtained ownership of the copyright." If any copyright claimant named in space 4 is not an author named in space 2, give a brief statement explaining how the claimant(s) obtained ownership of the copyright. Examples: "By written contract"; "Transfer of all rights by author"; "Assignment"; "By will." Do not attach transfer documents or other attachments or riders.

5 SPACE 5: Previous Registration

General Instructions: The questions in space 5 are intended to show whether an earlier registration has been made for this work and, if so, whether there is any basis for a new registration. As a general rule, only one basic copyright registration can be made for the same version of a particular work.

Same Version: If this version is substantially the same as the work covered by a previous registration, a second registration is not generally possible unless: (1) the work has been registered in unpublished form and a second registration is now being sought to cover this first published edition; or (2) someone other than the author is identified as copyright claimant in the earlier registration, and the author is now seeking registration in his or her own name. If either of these two exceptions apply, check the appropriate box and give the earlier registration number and date. Otherwise, do not submit Form PA; instead, write the Copyright Office for information about supplementary registration or recordation of transfers of copyright ownership.

Changed Version: If the work has been changed and you are now seeking registration to cover the additions or revisions, check the last box in space 5, give the earlier registration number and date, and complete both parts of space 6 in accordance with the instructions below.

Previous Registration Number and Date: If more than one previous registration has been made for the work, give the number and date of the latest registration.

6 SPACE 6: Derivative Work or Compilation

General Instructions: Complete space 6 if this work is a "changed version," "compilation," or "derivative work," and if it incorporates one or more earlier works that have already been published or registered for copyright or that have fallen into the public domain. A "compilation" is defined as "a work formed by the collection and assembling of preexisting materials or of data that are selected, coordinated, or arranged in such a way that the resulting work as a whole constitutes an original work of authorship." A "derivative work" is "a work based on one or more preexisting works." Examples of derivative works include musical arrangements, dramatizations, translations, abridgments, condensations, motion picture versions, or "any other form in which a work may be recast, transformed, or adapted." Derivative works also include works "consisting of editorial revisions, annotations, or other modifications" if these changes, as a whole, represent an original work of authorship.

Preexisting Material (space 6a): Complete this space **and** space 6b for derivative works. In this space identify the preexisting work that has been recast, transformed, or adapted. For example, the preexisting material might be: "French version of Hugo's 'Le Roi s'amuse'." Do not complete this space for compilations.

Material Added to This Work (space 6b): Give a brief, general statement of the **additional** new material covered by the copyright claim for which registration is sought. In the case of a derivative work, identify this new material. Examples: "Arrangement for piano and orchestra"; "Dramatization for television"; "New film version"; "Revisions throughout; Act III completely new." If the work is a compilation, give a brief, general statement describing both the material that has been compiled **and** the compilation itself. Example: "Compilation of 19th Century Military Songs."

7, 8, 9 SPACE 7, 8, 9: Fee, Correspondence, Certification, Return Address

Deposit Account: If you maintain a Deposit Account in the Copyright Office, identify it in space 7a. Otherwise, leave the space blank and send the fee of $20* (see box page 1) with your application and deposit.

Correspondence (space 7b): This space should contain the name, address, area code, telephone number, fax number, and email address (if available) of the person to be consulted if correspondence about this application becomes necessary.

Certification (space 8): The application cannot be accepted unless it bears the date and the **handwritten signature** of the author or other copyright claimant, or of the owner of exclusive right(s), or of the duly authorized agent of the author, claimant, or owner of exclusive right(s).

Address for Return of Certificate (space 9): The address box must be completed legibly since the certificate will be returned in a window envelope.

MORE INFORMATION

How to Register a Recorded Work: If the musical or dramatic work that you are registering has been recorded (as a tape, disk, or cassette), you may choose either copyright application Form PA (Performing Arts) or Form SR (Sound Recordings), depending on the purpose of the registration.

Form PA should be used to register the underlying musical composition or dramatic work. Form SR has been developed specifically to register a "sound recording" as defined by the Copyright Act—a work resulting from the "fixation of a series of sounds," separate and distinct from the underlying musical or dramatic work. Form SR should be used when the copyright claim is limited to the sound recording itself. (In one instance, Form SR may also be used to file for a copyright registration for both kinds of works—see (4) below.) Therefore:

(1) **File Form PA** if you are seeking to register the musical or dramatic work, not the "sound recording," even though what you deposit for copyright purposes may be in the form of a phonorecord.

(2) **File Form PA** if you are seeking to register the audio portion of an audiovisual work, such as a motion picture soundtrack; these are considered integral parts of the audiovisual work.

(3) **File Form SR** if you are seeking to register the "sound recording" itself, that is, the work that results from the fixation of a series of musical, spoken, or other sounds, but not the underlying musical or dramatic work.

(4) **File Form SR** if you are the copyright claimant for both the underlying musical or dramatic work and the sound recording, *and* you prefer to register both on the same form.

(5) **File both forms PA and SR** if the copyright claimant for the underlying work and sound recording differ, or you prefer to have separate registration for them.

"Copies" and "Phonorecords": To register for copyright, you are required to deposit "copies" or "phonorecords." These are defined as follows:

Musical compositions may be embodied (fixed) in "copies," objects from which a work can be read or visually perceived, directly or with the aid of a machine or device, such as manuscripts, books, sheet music, film, and videotape. They may also be fixed in "phonorecords," objects embodying fixations of sounds, such as tapes and phonograph disks, commonly known as phonograph records. For example, a song (the work to be registered) can be reproduced in sheet music ("copies") or phonograph records ("phonorecords"), or both.

FEE CHANGES
Registration filing fees are effective through June 30, 1999. For information on the fee changes, write the Copyright Office, check http://www.loc.gov/copyright, or call (202) 707-3000. Beginning as early as January 1, 2000, the Copyright Office may impose a service charge when insufficient fees are received.

FORM PA
For a Work of the Performing Arts
UNITED STATES COPYRIGHT OFFICE

REGISTRATION NUMBER

PA PAU

EFFECTIVE DATE OF REGISTRATION

Month Day Year

DO NOT WRITE ABOVE THIS LINE. IF YOU NEED MORE SPACE, USE A SEPARATE CONTINUATION SHEET.

1

TITLE OF THIS WORK ▼

PREVIOUS OR ALTERNATIVE TITLES ▼

NATURE OF THIS WORK ▼ See instructions

2

a NAME OF AUTHOR ▼ — DATES OF BIRTH AND DEATH: Year Born ▼ Year Died ▼

Was this contribution to the work a "work made for hire"? ☐ Yes ☐ No

AUTHOR'S NATIONALITY OR DOMICILE (Name of Country) OR { Citizen of ▶ / Domiciled in ▶ }

WAS THIS AUTHOR'S CONTRIBUTION TO THE WORK: Anonymous? ☐ Yes ☐ No; Pseudonymous? ☐ Yes ☐ No. If the answer to either of these questions is "Yes," see detailed instructions.

NATURE OF AUTHORSHIP Briefly describe nature of material created by this author in which copyright is claimed. ▼

b NAME OF AUTHOR ▼ — DATES OF BIRTH AND DEATH: Year Born ▼ Year Died ▼

Was this contribution to the work a "work made for hire"? ☐ Yes ☐ No

AUTHOR'S NATIONALITY OR DOMICILE (Name of Country) OR { Citizen of ▶ / Domiciled in ▶ }

WAS THIS AUTHOR'S CONTRIBUTION TO THE WORK: Anonymous? ☐ Yes ☐ No; Pseudonymous? ☐ Yes ☐ No. If the answer to either of these questions is "Yes," see detailed instructions.

NATURE OF AUTHORSHIP Briefly describe nature of material created by this author in which copyright is claimed. ▼

c NAME OF AUTHOR ▼ — DATES OF BIRTH AND DEATH: Year Born ▼ Year Died ▼

Was this contribution to the work a "work made for hire"? ☐ Yes ☐ No

AUTHOR'S NATIONALITY OR DOMICILE (Name of Country) OR { Citizen of ▶ / Domiciled in ▶ }

WAS THIS AUTHOR'S CONTRIBUTION TO THE WORK: Anonymous? ☐ Yes ☐ No; Pseudonymous? ☐ Yes ☐ No. If the answer to either of these questions is "Yes," see detailed instructions.

NATURE OF AUTHORSHIP Briefly describe nature of material created by this author in which copyright is claimed. ▼

NOTE
Under the law, the "author" of a "work made for hire" is generally the employer, not the employee (see instructions). For any part of this work that was "made for hire" check "Yes" in the space provided, give the employer (or other person for whom the work was prepared) as "Author" of that part, and leave the space for dates of birth and death blank.

3

a YEAR IN WHICH CREATION OF THIS WORK WAS COMPLETED — This information must be given in all cases. ◀ Year

b DATE AND NATION OF FIRST PUBLICATION OF THIS PARTICULAR WORK — Complete this information ONLY if this work has been published. Month ▶ Day ▶ Year ▶ ◀ Nation

4

COPYRIGHT CLAIMANT(S) Name and address must be given even if the claimant is the same as the author given in space 2. ▼

See instructions before completing this space.

TRANSFER If the claimant(s) named here in space 4 is (are) different from the author(s) named in space 2, give a brief statement of how the claimant(s) obtained ownership of the copyright. ▼

DO NOT WRITE HERE / OFFICE USE ONLY:
APPLICATION RECEIVED
ONE DEPOSIT RECEIVED
TWO DEPOSITS RECEIVED
FUNDS RECEIVED

MORE ON BACK ▶ • Complete all applicable spaces (numbers 5-9) on the reverse side of this page. • See detailed instructions. • Sign the form at line 8.

DO NOT WRITE HERE

Page 1 of ____ pages

EXAMINED BY FORM PA

CHECKED BY

CORRESPONDENCE
☐ Yes

FOR COPYRIGHT OFFICE USE ONLY

DO NOT WRITE ABOVE THIS LINE. IF YOU NEED MORE SPACE, USE A SEPARATE CONTINUATION SHEET.

5

PREVIOUS REGISTRATION Has registration for this work, or for an earlier version of this work, already been made in the Copyright Office?
☐ Yes ☐ No If your answer is "Yes," why is another registration being sought? (Check appropriate box.) ▼
a. ☐ This is the first published edition of a work previously registered in unpublished form.
b. ☐ This is the first application submitted by this author as copyright claimant.
c. ☐ This is a changed version of the work, as shown by space 6 on this application.
If your answer is "Yes," give: **Previous Registration Number ▼** **Year of Registration ▼**

6

DERIVATIVE WORK OR COMPILATION Complete both space 6a and 6b for a derivative work; complete only 6b for a compilation.
a **Preexisting Material** Identify any preexisting work or works that this work is based on or incorporates. ▼

See instructions before completing this space.

b **Material Added to This Work** Give a brief, general statement of the material that has been added to this work and in which copyright is claimed. ▼

7

a **DEPOSIT ACCOUNT** If the registration fee is to be charged to a Deposit Account established in the Copyright Office, give name and number of Account.
Name ▼ **Account Number ▼**

b **CORRESPONDENCE** Give name and address to which correspondence about this application should be sent. Name/Address/Apt/City/State/ZIP ▼

Area code and daytime telephone number ▶ ( ) Fax number ▶ ( )
Email ▶

8

CERTIFICATION* I, the undersigned, hereby certify that I am the
Check only one ▶
☐ author
☐ other copyright claimant
☐ owner of exclusive right(s)
☐ authorized agent of
Name of author or other copyright claimant, or owner of exclusive right(s) ▲

of the work identified in this application and that the statements made by me in this application are correct to the best of my knowledge.

Typed or printed name and date ▼ If this application gives a date of publication in space 3, do not sign and submit it before that date.

Date ▶

Handwritten signature (X) ▼

x

9

Mail certificate to:
Name ▼
Number/Street/Apt ▼
City/State/ZIP ▼

Certificate will be mailed in window envelope

YOU MUST:
• Complete all necessary spaces
• Sign your application in space 8

SEND ALL 3 ELEMENTS IN THE SAME PACKAGE:
1. Application form
2. Nonrefundable $20* filing fee in check or money order payable to *Register of Copyrights*
3. Deposit material

MAIL TO:
Library of Congress
Copyright Office
101 Independence Avenue, S.E.
Washington, D.C. 20559-6000

*Registration filing fees are effective through June 30, 1999. For the latest fee information, write the Copyright Office, check the Copyright Office Website at http://www.loc.gov/copyright, or call (202) 707-3000.

*17 U.S.C. § 506(e): Any person who knowingly makes a false representation of a material fact in the application for copyright registration provided for by section 409, or in any written statement filed in connection with the application, shall be fined not more than $2,500.

July 1998—70,000
WEB REV: July 1998
PRINTED ON RECYCLED PAPER
☆U.S. GOVERNMENT PRINTING OFFICE: 1998-432-381/80,012

Some singer/songwriters get their start by writing songs for others. This is referred to as horizontal writing. Writing a song you sing yourself is known as vertical writing. Horizontal writing is the hardest because you have to write for a variety of voices and styles, and will have to convince the publisher (one who shops your songs to others) that your song is commercially marketable. As a vertical writer you will have the opportunity to be more artistically creative, and will deal with record companies that may be looking for your unique sound. Vertical writers earn more money and if the song becomes a hit, will continue to earn income for a number of years to come.

Most people love a good love song, just as most people love a good love story. Sometimes someone writes a love song that may be picked up by Hollywood and used in a film, such as "When a Man Loves a Women," which was heard in the movie "Ghost." Both the song and film were instant smash hits. A well-written ballad sung by the right artist—one who knows how to sing the lyrics and music with feeling—is always a winner.

Study the hits of the past and analyze what made them work. Writers that make it are ones that can feel, tell a story, understand how to formulate musical notes to best express emotion, are confident in themselves, keep writing no matter how many rejections they get, turn disappointment into creativity, and keep right on learning the art of songwriting.

And remember: If you do become a songwriter, copyright your material before showing it to anyone.

COPYRIGHTS

A copy right is the exclusive right to reproduce, publish, and sell the matter and form of a literary musical or artistic work. Copyrighting protects you, against others plagiarizing your work. Titles and ideas can not be copyrighted.

According to the 1976 Copyright Law, work put into a fixed form is copyrighted automatically, but to copyright your work officially, send twenty dollars and a completed PA Form (Performing Arts form) to the Copyright Office, Library of Congress, Washington, D.C. 20559 to register your work. (See PA form in this chapter.)

To call for forms and for the circular number, dial (202) 707-9100. Keep a blank form for your files. You are permitted to make blank copies for future use. Send two copies of your phonorecord (tape or video), along with the form PA and your check or money order. If you have any questions you may call the public information number, (202) 707-3000.

After you copyright your material, you will want to join one or more music organizations.

MUSIC ORGANIZATIONS

Nashville's Songwriters Association (NSA) is an organization for the non-published writer. They offer an associate membership and a variety of help to the novice writer. For additional information write to:

NSA, Int'l
1701 Westend Ave
Nashville, TN 37203
(615) 256-3354

Songwriters Guild of America (SGA) was founded in 1931, for and by songwriters. Both published and unpublished songwriters may become members. SGA offers many services and is run by volunteers. Members receive help with contracts, publishing concerns, health insurance plans, copyright renewals, and estates of songwriters who are no longer living. The songwriters guild offers workshops on a variety of subjects pertaining to the business of songwriting. For information on membership, write to the office of your music city choice.

SGA
1516 Broadway
Suite 36
New York, NY 10060
(212) 768-7902

SGA
6430 Sunset Blvd
Suite 705
Hollywood, CA 90028
(213) 462-1108

SGA
1222 16th Avenue South
Suite 25
Nashville, TN 37212
(615) 329-1782
Or browse the SGA website at: http://www.songwriters.org.

National Academy of Songwriters (NAS) is a song bank where writers can establish ownership and date the creation of their song. Songwriters get immediate protection by registering with NAS, while copyright registration can take a few months. The NAS and copyright registrations will both hold up in court if a dispute of ownership arises. NAS costs ten dollars for members for the first song and two dollars for each additional song registered at the same time. NAS keeps the songs registered for ten years, at which time members may renew. Write to:

NAS
6255 Sunset Blvd
Suite 1023
Hollywood California 90028
(213) 463-7178
NAS website is: www.nassong.org

Academy of Country Music (ACM) was established in 1964 to promote country music. Any person involved in the business or creative aspect of country music may become a member. This organization offers seminars, showcases, and other country music events. For additional information write to:

ACM
PO Box 508
Hollywood, CA 90078
(213) 462-2351
ACM website is: acmcountry.com

The Country Music Association (CMA) is listed on page 100 of this book.

Nashville Songwriters Association International (NSAI) was established in 1967 for professional and amateur songwriters. Members receive help in legal and business matters, as well as songwriting techniques. For information on NSAI write to:

NSAI
1701 Westend Ave.
Nashville, TN 37203
(615) 256-3354
NSAI website is: www.songs.org.

American Society of Composers, Authors, and Publishers (ASCAP), founded in 1914, is a nonprofit organization that is owned by its more than 75,000 members of composers, songwriters, lyricists, and music publishers. ASCAP keeps track of songwriters and publishers material by way of a performance survey. The surveys cover performances on AM/FM public and college radio; local network, public and cable television; airlines; MUZAK and similar background music services; live performances in symphony and concert halls; colleges and universities; and a wide range of other live venues. They collect royalties from these venues—around the world—and pay a percentage to the composer, author, and publisher. It not only collects and distributes royalties to members, it helps by conducting workshops, having showcases, keeping information current on a website, sending a free publication "Playback," and offering a member card with a full-range of benefits. The three main offices are:

ASCAP
1 Lincoln Plaza
New York, NY 10023
(212) 621-6000

ASCAP
2 Music Square West
Nashville, TN 37203
(615) 742-5000

ASCAP
7920 Sunset Blvd
Suite 300
Hollywood, CA 90046
(323) 883-1000
Or browse the ASCAP websites at: www.ascap.com.

The ASCAP foundation was made possible due to a donation made by the widow of a songwriter—Jack Norworth (author of "Take Me Out To the Ballgame," and "Shine on Harvest Moon.") Because of the Norworth family, a grants program was instituted for young composers. This program was just the beginning. ASCAP Foundation has scholarship programs, and gives awards and grants to songwriters, composers, musicians, and students at all levels. The Foundation can be reached by calling: (212) 621-6219 or by browsing their website at: www.ascapfoundation.org. Broadcast Music, Inc. (BMI) was founded in 1940 by the National Association of Broadcasters and is a major performing rights society. BMI has over 160,000 songwriters, composers and music publishers as members. BMI keeps track of performances by way of sampling radio. Radio stations keep logs of music played. Television reports to BMI by way of music cue sheets. BMI pays royalties according to their schedule sheet. Each member has a payment schedule sheet, and they know when to expect payment. Members may attend musical theatre workshops, film and television workshops, and jazz composers workshops. They also receive the BMI magazine—"BMI Music World," and may receive an award for the student composers competition. To encourage and aid young composers of concert music, BMI and the BMI Foundation, annually hold the competition and presents cash awards to the winners. The three main offices are:

BMI
320 West 57 Street
New York, NY 10019
(212) 536-2000

BMI
10 Music Square East
Nashville, TN 37203
(615) 401-2000

BMI
8730 Sunset Blvd
Third-floor West
Hollywood, CA 90069
(310) 659-9109
Or browse the BMI websites at: bmi.com

The Society of European Stage Artists and Composers (SESAC) was founded in 1931 and has both writers and publishers as members. SESAC tracks in much the same way as the other two performing rights organizations. It is the smallest of the three organizations, but states that what it lacks in size, is made up by more individual attention to members. Two main offices are:

SESAC
421 West 54th Street
New York, NY 10019
(212) 586-3450

SESAC
55 Music Square East
Nashville, TN 37203
(615) 320-0055
Or browse the SESAC websites at: http;\sesac.com

You will want to join ASCAP, BMI, or SESAC if you have a commerical song you wrote or published, because that's how you get paid rights and royalties. Contact each of the three organizations and request a packet. When you receive the information, read it carefully and select the organization that best suits your needs.

The aspiring singer should also know about the Harry Fox Agency. It was established in 1927 by the National Music Publishers' Association for the sole purpose of providing service for licensing musical copyrights. This agency handles the collection and distribution of royalties for music publishers. Before a singer records the works of another songwriter, he will have to acquire the rights from the Harry Fox Agency if the writer's publisher is listed with them. When you contact the publisher, he will tell you if he is signed with the Harry Fox Agency. If so, contact the agency by writing to:

The Harry Fox Agency, Inc.
711 3rd Ave. 8th Flr.
New York, NY 10017
(212) 370-5330
Harry Fox Agency website is: www.harryfox.com.

SHOWCASES FOR SONGWRITERS

If you write songs and would like an opportunity to showcase your work in Nashville, send a tape to the Bluebird Cafe, listed on page 98. If they are interested, you will hear from them. Be sure to include your phone number and address. Every Monday night the Blue Bird Cafe holds an open-mike night. If you are in the area and would like to perform you need to sign-up by 5:45 PM. Be sure to arrive early, because there is usually a long waiting line and the drawing starts at 6 PM. Twenty-five names are selected at random. If you are selected, you will perform two original songs. If you are not selected, and can come back, put your name in basket-2; if you are on the previous list your chances are better. One reason songwriters would want to showcase at the Blue Bird Cafe is the exposure to the music business people who often show up in the audience.

For showcases in other music cities, call the Chamber of Commerce or Visitor's Center in your area of interest.

PITCHING SONGS TO PUBLISHERS

When pitching songs to publishers, act professional and keep things neat and simple. Use quality cassettes or CD's. The songs should be positive and up tempo, although you can make an exception to this if you've written a strong ballad. You will also need to type a professional looking lyric sheet (no hand written corrections), organized by verse, chorus, bridge or whatever format you choose. Be sure to include the title of the song, your copyright notice, and your name and phone number. Send the tape of the one to three songs you are pitching. Also make sure to label the tape with the title, copyright notice, name and phone number; include the cue at the start of the song. Fold the lyric sheet in half (twice) and attach it to the back of the cassette with a rubber band around the sides of the cassette. Do not send the plastic tape container and do not put the tape/folded sheet in anything other than a padded envelope. Include a SASE (a self addressed stamped envelope, with correct postage for envelope and cassette weight.

Occasionally songwriters can get their songs to an industry person themselves, but usually a reputable publisher is needed. If you are that unique individual lucky enough to find a publisher who is interested in your song, things can start happening. The publisher will have your demo polished and will pitch it to major artists. Remember, when pitching to publishers, be professional and KISS (keep it simple songwriter).

You can find a reputable publisher by asking other industry people, looking on the backs of albums, contacting ASCAP or BMI, and checking with other music associations. Another way to locate reputable publishers is to check the music charts for active publishers who handle your type of music. You can get their addresses and telephone numbers from the Billboard's International Buyers Guide. Billboard is an annual publication that can be found at your local library. There is one other way to find publishers for your songwriting: The Writer's Digest, an organization for all types of writers has published a book entitled, "Song Writer's Market." There are over 500 pages listing over 2,000 names and addresses of songwriting publishers. To purchase the book, write or call:

Writer's Digest Books
1507 Dana Avenue
Cincinnati, Ohio 45206
(513) 531-8250

Or browse their website at: www.writer's digest.com.

When you find the right publisher, call for an appointment and drop the tape off, if possible. Try to see the Director of A & R (artists and repertoire), or the person in charge of artist relations. Work as close to the top as possible. Because of infringement laws, publishers rarely accept unsolicited material. They usually work through trusted contacts. You will be lucky if you are permitted to leave your tape with the secretary or receptionist, so be polite and grateful if they accept it from you. Every time you have a new demo, make the rounds again. Be optimistic, but realistic.

It is a tough road to go, but learn something from each experience and keep working toward your goal. It is important to connect with a publisher with real business savvy and with the clout to make things happen.

Before pitching to publishers, ask yourself why you like the particular song(s). Listen to the lyrics, melody, arrangement, vocals, guitar, rhythm, the chorus, and the verses. Do you have a strong hook? Even though music and lyrics are vitally important, a hook is what really sells a song.

If your song is published and receives airplay and doesn't make the top ten, study the songs that do, and ask yourself which ones move you emotionally. Then figure out what you can do next time to spark an emotional response in yourself and others. Ask publishers what they would like to hear.

When you do manage to get your tape into the hands of a publisher and one of the songs is a commercially marketable product, the publisher will probably want to secure a contract with you. You can sign exclusively with that publisher and he or she will start a catalog of songs for you. Or you can sign a single-song contract with a clause that specifies the song reverts back to you after a certain date. If you sign exclusively and the song becomes a hit, the catalog becomes valuable. That's why some writers and singer/songwriters form their own publishing companies after they start writing hits.

You definitely can make more money by self-publishing, especially if you are both writer and recording artist, but it's better to wait until you become an established writer before doing so.

To publish your own songs, join ASCAP, BMI or SESAC. Form yourself as a company or as a partner with a reputable publisher or collaborator. Seek the advice of your entertainment attorney.

COLLABORATION

If you write lyrics but not melody, collaborate with a music writer. Don't hide away a good song because you don't want to share the rewards. After all, where would Rodgers have been without Hammerstein? Lerner without Lowe? If you decide to collaborate, you must, of course, indicate that collaboration on the copyright form. Teaming with another person can lead to rewards, both artistically and financially.

Record companies pay royalties based on sales (mechanicals). Licensing companies (ASCAP, BMI or SESAC) pay a royalty based on usage. You also get paid royalties from sheet music sales and by synchronization license (commercials or movies). So if your song is a hit, you could both be making money for a number of years.

You can find a collaborator by going to places where writers hang out—restaurants, clubs, writing seminars, writing classes, writing organizations—or you can place an ad in a music publication.

If you have written some great lyrics and need someone to set music to them, you can also look for private music instructors, church musical directors, and performing musicians by contacting the local chapter of the American Federation of Musicians (AFM), a musicians' union. There are AFM offices in most large cities.

When interviewing collaborators, make sure they are as serious about writing and learning as you are. Ask about work schedules, work habits, interest level, and what they expect out of the collaborative effort.

Do not pay a collaborator. Instead both of you promote and pitch the song to publishers. The publisher will pay you both.

The publisher will want to know your writing agreements, so decide up front—and in writing—how earnings will be shared, who has the right to change the song, what happens if the song isn't published successfully, and what happens if the writing collaboration ends. This is a good time to seek advice from your entertainment attorney. It is wise for each of you to have your own attorney.

BEWARE

Be careful about falling for ads that ask you for money to publish your poems, your music, or any part of your writing. If the publisher is reputable, you shouldn't have to front any money. Don't share song ideas with anyone until you have the song in writing and have protected yourself legally. I know that friends often mull around ideas, but if you are serious about the song be cautious with it.

CHAPTER 16

RECORD CONTRACT

The beginning singer usually will need a record contract before being asked to perform on television or in films. Good managers know this and spend a great deal of time trying to land a record deal for their artists. The manager will work from the top down—at a record company, a publisher's office, or with an entertainment attorney—to make this happen. Finally it will happen and you will have a signed record contract. Does this mean that you are on your way? Not necessarily. All this means is that you have a recording contract. That is very exciting, but keep your goals in mind and stay focused. You are not a star yet, but you have climbed further on the ladder to success. Now that record has to sell. Your family and friends will make a big deal of it, and they should, but if the general public won't buy the recording, you aren't going anywhere.

This is where you take everything you have learned about stage presence, the audience, and professionalism and show the record company that you are the best thing that has ever happened to them. Your manager has to encourage the record company to give you the heavy promotion you deserve, and will convince them that you will live up to the contract. If you can prove that you are one talented, responsible, polished entertainer, the record company will want to produce and market you and you will soon be on your way to stardom.

Before signing with a record company, have an entertainment attorney review the contract. He will check it over for length of contract, options, record releases, who owns rights to what, what kinds of royalties will be paid, percentage of royalties to each, advances offered (for record deals, videos, tours, promotions), special request clauses, and any other information pertaining to the contract. The contract can become complicated by the interpretation of one word, so know what you are signing.

RECORD COMPANIES

There are well over a thousand record companies in the United States and over two thousand labels. (Some companies have subsidiary labels.)

There are small to large independent labels and the highly sought after major labels. The aspiring singer will usually work with the smaller label first, sometimes sharing the costs of the recording by way of a financial backer. But because you are shooting for superstardom, you will strive to work with companies such as Arista and the major labels (the elites). You are well on your way to becoming successful when one of the elite record companies believes you have talent and that you will make money for them. The elite companies will not ask you for up-front monies. They will assume all initial publishing, recording, promotion, and other financial risks. They pay artists or songwriters by cash payments or royalties and they copyright recordings and publications in their company name and pay all expenses. The elite companies will work with artists only if they can predict future profits on them. This is why it is important to be commercially ready before approaching an elite company.

The larger record companies offer stability and strong promotion and distribution. They are organized by various departments: The Administration Department handles all business and legal matters, including publishing and international affairs. The Artist Relations Department handles anything that directly relates to the artist. The Production, the Creative Services, the Manufacturing, the Promotion, and the Distribution Departments handle everything from producing, merchandising, mass duplication and publicity, to mass distribution. Each department is separate from the other, and there are many people interacting to accomplish the final goals of the company. It is a fast-paced complex business. Because of this, it is essential to have a knowledgeable and reputable manager.

The major record companies want you to have a business manager. They prefer to talk to you about music and to your manager about business items. Major record companies cannot afford the time to train you in the art of business. A representative of the label will want to see you perform live. If you sound good on a record, but can't excite an audience, you probably won't sell the recording. You also will not sell yourself to the label. See how important the basics become. Review Part II before pitching to a label and be ready. The major labels like to see, as well as hear, originality in song and style.

If you haven't found a reputable manager, and you've taken all of the right steps, then produce the best tape or video you can afford and call the label company to see if it is accepting new material. Drop by the record company and ask if you may leave your tape.

If you do get signed and have your act together, it is in the record company's best interest to do everything in its power to help make you a star. It will get your face and name out to the masses and will create avenues for hype.

The record company will produce you on a professional master recording, select the best song from the recording and have you perform it in a music video, and heavily promote you on the radio, television, and on tours.

Record companies can do a lot to establish your career, but the final outcome depends upon you.

MASTER RECORDING

A master recording is a top notch representation of the vocals, instruments, strings, and effects. It is a quality marketable product. Because it is a marketable product, and it may be performed on radio or television, this might be the time to consider joining AFTRA (discussed later). Master recordings should be recorded under the American Federation of Television and Radio Artists (AFTRA) code, which states that when a record company acquires the rights to a master recording from an outside source, the record company must furnish AFTRA with a warranty and representation that all performances included in the master were recorded in the United States, or its territories and possessions (recording territory). It also states that all artists have been paid the minimum rates in effect at the time of the recording under the AFTRA code, and that all payments due to the AFTRA pension and welfare funds have been made. This is an extremely complex area. Most major record companies have their own production studios and adhere to the AFTRA codes, and most artists become a member of AFTRA before vocalizing on a master recording.

The record company will assign its in-house producer to the production of your master recording. The production process is accomplished in three stages; pre-production, in-the-studio, and post-production.

The pre-production stage is one of creating the ideas, working out the budget, scheduling all parties and equipment involved, song selection, handling mechanical licenses, and working out the musical arrangement.

The in-the-studio stage is the actual laying down of the tracks, mixing the tracks, distributing the employee forms and collecting them, deciding on potential singles, and making several copies of the finished product for the artist and producer.

The post-production stage is the supervising of the master recording, working with others on the cover design and other graphics, submitting the W-4 forms and licenses, lyric sheets, and technical credits to the record company. This stage of production is where everyone gets paid and the master tape is hand-carried to the A&R department. This master recording can cost well over $100,000.

AFTRA is a national union affiliated with the AFL-CIO with its headquarters in New York. I talked with AFTRA and was given the words they wanted me to write. Its members consist of professional actors, vocalists, radio personalities, television personalities, puppeteers, and other performing artists.

The purpose of AFTRA is to negotiate and enforce contracts (locally and nationally), continuously improve on wages and working conditions, and establish minimum union scales for its members. Union scales are minimum professional wages that one is paid for doing a specific duty—the bargaining base.

There are other advantages of joining AFTRA: the retirement plan, the health plans, residual payments (for repeated broadcasts), safety and environmental conditions while on the job, arbitrators to handle grievances, job security, and standard time off (vacations and holidays). Also, members receive the AFTRA magazine which keeps them up-to-date on important entertainment concerns.

An AFTRA office can be found in most large cities throughout the United States. Some form of AFTRA has been in existence since 1919 and most reputable record companies have signed an AFTRA agreement. When you perform for a recording session, make sure the producer is signed and his signature is on the member report along with his address and telephone number.

An AFTRA singer may work for local non-signatory producers up to four times in Nashville (a right-to-work state), but cannot work for non-signatory producers in New York and LA. When you do work for a non-signatory producer you will be working under a letter of adherence (limited letter). After the limited one or four productions, the producer will be asked to sign a full contract with AFTRA for future projects.

An AFTRA member cannot be represented by a talent agent who is not a union franchised agent. A union franchised talent agent has met AFTRA's finance and business work ethics requirements. These agents may not charge an artist more than 10 percent interest and will assist the artist in AFTRA's rules and regulations.

Some singers go on to appear in films and will eventually become members of the Screen Actors Guild (SAG). The same rules that apply to AFTRA applies to SAG. Some talent agents are members of both AFTRA and SAG. In Nashville some local booking agencies that represent recording artists and are franchised to AFTRA and SAG are:

TML, Inc.
4516 Granny White Pike
Nashville, TN 37204
(615) 321-5596

Buddy Lee Attractions
38 Music Square East
Nashville, TN 37203
(615) 244-4336

Creative Artists Agency
3310 West End Avenue
5th floor
Nashville, TN 37203
(615) 383-8787

William Morris Agency
2100 Westend Ave.
Suite 1000
Nashville, TN 37203
(615) 963-3000

AFTRA members must fill out a member report for all recording sessions. The member report is a form which lists the time, place, date, and type of work performed. The member report must be filed with the local AFTRA office within ten working days.

Each AFTRA locals are governed by their own set of rules and regulations, but all locals are open unions and do not discriminate against any person based on race, creed, color, national origin, religion, or sexual orientation.

Once a singer is an AFTRA member and is booked by a signatory agency, the venue booking contract reflects the proper representation. At some level of success you will want to become a member of AFTRA in the music city of your choice. For more information and a membership package write to:

AFTRA
1108-17th Avenue South
Nashville, TN 37212
(615) 327-2944

For the Nashville-based AFTRA, there is a one time initiation fee and local dues every six months. Check with the Nashville AFTRA office for current costs and additional information. To request a membership packet write to:

AFTRA
260 Madison Avenue
New York, NY 10016
(212) 532-0800

For the New York based AFTRA, there is an initial fee to join, and local dues every six months. Check with the New York City

AFTRA office for current costs and additional information on membership requirements.

There are far too many talent agencies that are franchised to the NYC AFTRA/SAG to list in this book. You can obtain the information, for a minimal fee, by writing to: Ross Reports, Television, 1515 Broadway, New York, NY 10036, or by calling (212) 764-7300.

AFTRA
5757 Wilshire Blvd
Ninth-Floor
Los Angeles, CA 90036
(323) 634-8100

To join the Los Angeles AFTRA union you will have to go into the office in person and fill out an application. You will pay an initial fee and the first six months of local dues. Bi-annual dues will be paid for the duration of membership. No personal checks will be accepted. You may pay by Visa, Master Card, cashier's check, or money order. Contact the local Los Angeles AFTRA office for current costs and any additional requirements.

AFTRA continuously studies the national and international markets. It oversees rapidly changing technology, legislation, shifting corporate ownership patterns and globalization of the industry in behalf of their members. You can browse the AFTRA website at: www.aftra.org.

THE CHARTS

You have signed with a major label, probably joined AFTRA, and have completed your first big-time recording session. This is where the charts become very important.

After the record has had airplay and makes it to the market, the record company professionals watch the rating charts to see if the song they are promoting falls onto the charts. If it hits the charts, they pay close attention where it falls within the 100 song range. A weak song (lacking in public appeal) doesn't stay on the charts very long. If a weak song does make it to the charts it won't be very profitable and all involved loses in time and money. On the other hand, a strong song that makes it to the charts and continues to climb usually has mass appeal and, if promoted properly is profitable for all those involved. A record release that climbs quickly is given a bullet.

A bullet means the record is gaining approximately five or six chart positions each week. That is a good indication the record may climb to the top of the charts.

Once the single makes it to the top it is recorded on an album. It is assumed that people will buy the whole album in order to own that one hit song. To encourage the mass audience to buy the album, the single is played on the radio and a visual (video) is produced for television.

All professionals use Billboard, Cashbox, and The Gavin Report, the three top trade magazines, to track the top 100 records and to keep up with a variety of information on the music business. Check your full-service book stores to purchase them.

MUSIC VIDEOS

The best advice on music videos is: Don't do one until you have developed yourself and your act to as close to perfection as you can manage, since for many people, your video will be the first and most lasting impression they get of you. Remember, when you do perform in a video, let the director do his job. You are not going to select a studio unless you have previously reviewed its work and liked it, so if you have artistic control, let the technical people do the work they are used to doing day after day. When you know you are ready for a lasting visual and have backing from a personal investor or a record company, hire a reputable video company and let the company produce your visual.

Music videos are a form of promotion—they are made to sell records. Of course, you'll use them to aid in acquiring agents, managers, and performing dates as well.

Because creating visualizations of individual songs has become an accepted marketing tool for selling records, the record company will usually risk the financing once you are signed to its label. The label will decide which single to produce as a music video. The label experts usually choose the one the radio stations will get and they are usually responsible for production and promotion. The record label will expect to recoup half of the cost from the artist through the sale of cassettes and compact discs before he or she is paid any royalties.

Record companies usually have the right to exploit the video in all entertainment markets, and they usually own the video copyrights. The artist is usually involved in the concept and in the selection of the director and production company. Even though the record company is assuming initial risks, it realizes you have a lot at stake as well. You've learned your craft; now it's vital that you be an astute team-player.

Music videos can range anywhere from a professional low-budget of $20,000-30,000 to a high budget for superstars of $500,000-plus. It's possible to produce a music video for less than $20,000, but most professional production companies charge at least this amount. Most low-budget music video productions are financed by the artist, or financial investor. Once it is completed it can be used as a promotional tool for clubs, MTV, managers, agents, or pitching to record companies.

The best avenue to market music videos is television. Music videos can be seen on cable television: MTV, VH-1, and Black Entertainment Television, as well as on the jukebox network, the Nashville network, country music television and broadcast television (NBC's Friday Night Videos and TBS's Night Tracks).

MUSIC VIDEO PRODUCERS

The music video producer is the overall director. He is responsible for locating a studio, hiring the engineer and musicians, and for the final outcome of the visualization and quality of sound. If you are financing your own video, look in the yellow pages under "Production" and check the backs of album covers at the video shops. Call the record label, or video production studio, and ask how to locate the producer you are interested in. Usually the major producers won't work with unknowns, but try anyway. If they choose not to work with you, they may suggest someone else for you.

Major record companies work with music video producers who belong to the Music Video Producer's Association. The MVPA is an organization that exchanges technical information and standardizes production bidding procedures and guidelines for fees and payment schedules.

Record companies advance money to the production company. They recoup this advanced money by taking 50 percent of the artist's record royalties, and usually 50 percent of the artist's net receipts from the exploitation of commercial markets. Net receipts are the gross video production costs, distribution fees and expenses, as well as payments to others involved. After 50 percent has been recouped by the record company, the artist will see earned income. Sometimes the record company will advance monies to the artist. When this happens, the record company recoups the advanced monies by taking either a larger percentage or will take the 50 percent for a longer period of time.

The greater the reputation of the producer, the more you or the record company will pay for the music video. You, or the record company, may be required to pay points. For example, three points equals 3 percent of gross earnings. It's worth paying points, however, to get the right producer, who can talk to the labels, managers, and other music business executives.

Music videos are important to the advancement of the singer's career, so the basics of choreography and acting techniques are invaluable.

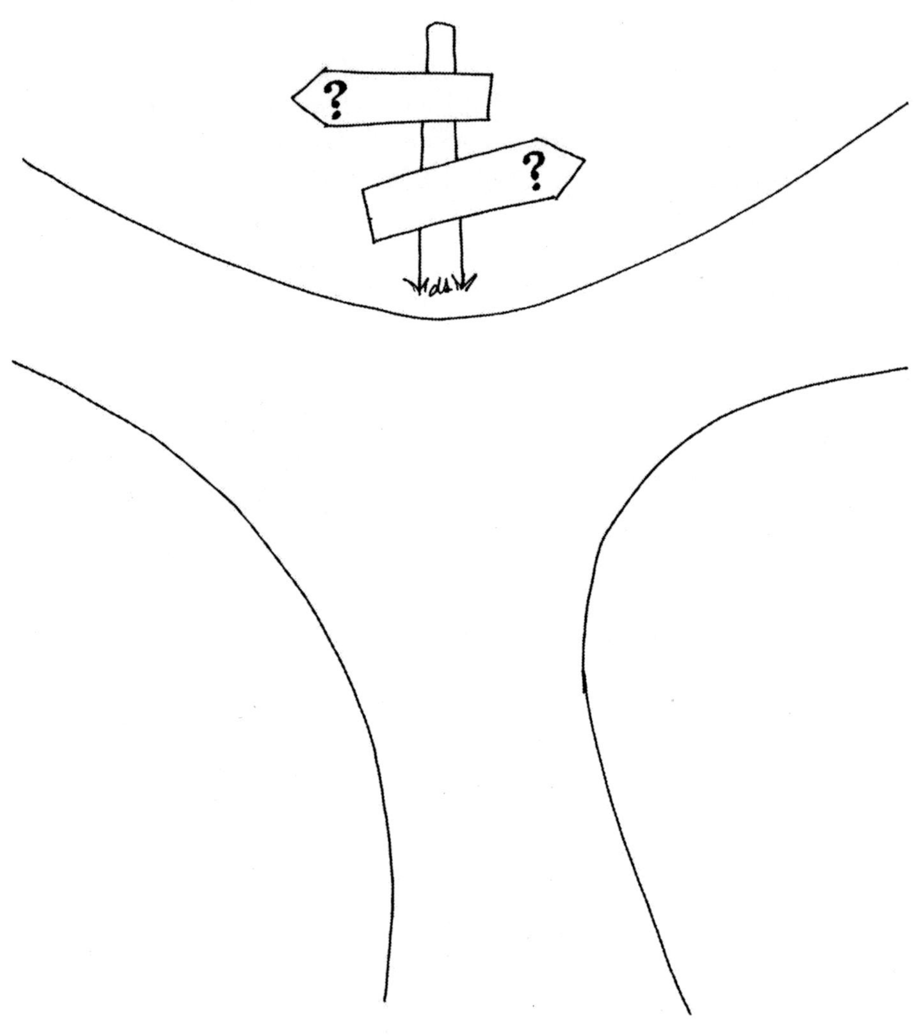

CHAPTER 17

ALTERNATE ROUTES

EDUCATION

If learning the ropes and developing your talent at home aren't for you, then another way to go is to get an education at a university with a music degree program. This way you will learn your craft through books and by performing on campus. An advantage of going this route is the internship program. As part of your degree training, you may have the opportunity to work for credit in the music industry in one of the major music cities. As part of your course of study you will live and work for several weeks at a job in the music field. You will be learning the trade and making an income. You will meet industry people, get to know the area, and maybe even get hired by the company you intern with as soon as you graduate. Perhaps a classmate has already graduated and moved to your desired area; could he or she use a roommate to help with expenses?

You now have two choices; which road will you take? Either way you go, the same basic principles will apply and you will always need to network. You will still need talent, team playing abilities, and all the tenacity you can muster.

PUBLICISTS AND PROMOTERS

If you are sure that one of your songs will be a hit, but you just cannot get your foot in the right door, consider hiring a publicity firm and three reputable promoters to do it for you. You can find music publicity firms and promoters by looking in the phone book, the Music Directory, and by asking your music contacts.

Expect to pay a few thousand dollars for the right people. Get your song promoted heavily for about six weeks and see what happens.

Does your song have a memorable hook? Is the melody line one that just won't leave your head? Is the song easy to dance to and is it fun? Could a new dance step be created for it? If you can answer yes, then publicists and promoters will be interested in hearing it, but only if your voice has quality and you have a unique style.

First, hire a publicist. Second, hire a tape or CD duplicator to make bulk copies of the one song you will be promoting for the radio (Check your source directories under "duplicators.") Third, hire the three top promoters in the area (Get recommendations from the publicist.) The better promoters have the ability to reach the top radio stations which could give your record airplay.

The publicist can get you promoted in the music trade magazines both in and outside of the United States, as well as promotion in other types of media. If you find a reputable publicist, he or she will tell you if you are marketable. after all, publicists have their own reputations to consider as well.

If you can get airplay and your record creates hype, you'll hear form the record companies. Hiring your own publicist and promoters is not the recommended way to go, but if you strongly believe in yourself that much, it could be worth a try.

WINNERS

> ...You can not squeeze 38-hours into a 24-hour day.
> ...it is okay to say "no" to some things.
>
> -Ty Herndon

It is important not to get frustrated. If a music career is what you must have, then keep going. Stay focused, but allow yourself some fun. When you feel discouraged, go to a movie, empty your head, forget about things for a day, treat yourself to a good dinner at a fine restaurant—anything to get you away from the struggle for a few hours. Get plenty of rest and exercise, and remember that you are an okay person. Surround yourself with those that love you—the real people—your family and close friends.

Once you collect yourself you'll feel better. Your attitude will stay positive, your energy will be revitalized, and you will be ready to handle the success that follows. And it will follow.

Winners never give up; they may take time out, but they never give up. Are you a winner? If you are, then you have one more step to climb. This is the step which will both make and keep you a superstar.

The last step on the aspiring singer's climb to superstardom is knowing what to do when you become the big "S"—SUPERSTAR—at the top of the musical staircase.

SUMMARY OF PART III

AFTER RELOCATING YOU WILL NEED TO:

- Network with music industry people
- Locate agents/manager/attorney/financial backer
- Record a professional demo
- Try songwriting
- Follow industry music charts
- Pitch to record companies
- Consider making a music video
- Hire publicist and promoters (a last resort)
- Be a winner

Congratulations. You have worked very hard and sacrificed much to achieve this level of accomplishment. Now, as Grath Brooks once said, "the real work has just begun"—Staying on top.

PART IV

STAYING ON TOP

CHAPTER 18

♪

AFTER YOU'VE MADE IT

...Once you're at the top, it's a long
way to the bottom and it's a fast fall."
-Loretta Lynn

KNOW YOUR ROAD CREW

It is important to know who is working for you, from the road crew to the road manager. You'll want and need dependable, trustworthy people with the right attitude. Imagine the frustration and embarrassment of performing at a particular venue, and then discovering that your road manager insulted or assaulted the promoter who hired you, one of your musicians "accidentally" took another band's equipment, or that your roadie did something less than desirable. These things have happened to others, and if something similar happens to you, it could be the end of your career; word gets around. Know the people you hire by checking references, by asking others in the business, and by being observant. Your reputation could depend on it.

You have to know when to dismiss people: For consistently being late to rehearsals and performances, not taking rehearsals and performances seriously, for dishonesty, for consistently bringing down the bands' morale, drug or alcohol abuse, for being argumentative at performances, and any other consistent negative behavior. Sometimes it truly is an attitude adjustment that is needed, but sometimes it could be a personal problem such as a family break-up, serious family illness, or the death of a family member or a very close friend. If your musician is normally a dedicated talented person, and one of these personal elements is the real source of the problem, then give this musician a temporary break. There are other musicians that you could hire for a few weeks. Take care of business, but be human.

MOTOR COACH

You can purchase a beautiful motor coach for you and your crew for $300,000 and up, or can rent one for around $450 plus, a day. Prices will vary depending on where you purchase or rent. You will want a 40 foot long, 8 foot wide, self-contained motor home.

When you reach star status you will need two buses—one for the band and equipment, and one for you and any family members.

AWARDS AND FANS

When you do make it to the top and you finally earn an award nomination, celebrate. Scream, jump around, tell everyone you know. Then calm down and make some plans. Make sure you know the date and time the award will be presented. Then find out where your nomination fits into the schedule, and who your contact person will be.

Prepare a brief acceptance speech and remember to thank the fans. Do not go over your allotted time thanking every person you know. Look pleasant, wear colors that complement, and remember that the camera is your friend.

In advance, let me congratulate you on your award. You have arrived and should feel very proud of your accomplishments. But never get too comfortable. You now have to climb the rest of the way to superstardom. Never stop reaching and never stop growing in other areas of the entertainment business. As Garth Brooks once said, "Now you have to work harder, because more is expected of you." He also reminds you to be loyal to your fans. Brooks believes that fan loyalty means selling them quality merchandise, giving them a quality performance, and being receptive to their needs. Garth says, "When you do make it, remember who is going to keep you there."

He practices what he preaches. I was working a concert featuring Garth and two other top performers at Bull Run in Manassas, Virginia one year, and shortly after the show was over, the other two performers left. Garth Brooks had his road manager reschedule a flight to his next performance and stayed until every last person had an autograph and a picture taken with him. I heard him tell his road manager that he wasn't leaving "until everyone that paid to see him gets an autograph, if they want one." That's one reason why Garth became the superstar he is.

Elvis Presley was another superstar. I know of no other entertainer who affected the emotions of people the way Elvis did, and still does today. A year or two before he met his untimely death, I was at one of his Sunday afternoon concerts in Washington, D.C. Elvis was tired. He had performed the night before and had been on the road all night to get to the concert. When he sang the "American Trilogy" he knew he wasn't up to par. After finishing the song, he said to the audience, "You deserve better than this. I can do better. Let me give you what you paid to hear. I will do it again". And he did. The audience was so moved by his generosity they gave him a standing ovation that lasted for what seemed an eternity. Real superstars know where their livelihood comes from, and they give back in full measure.

It all comes back to the basics—take care of those who take care of you and the rest will take care of itself.

CHAPTER 19

WOMEN IN THE BUSINESS

...If you're going to be in the music
business, why not make a mark...
- Tina Turner

I can not write this book without giving credit to all the women who have made their mark and paved the rough road of success, which has made it a little easier for the talented females of today to travel it behind them. Among them are Patsy Cline, Patsy Montana, Kitty Wells, Lynn Anderson, Judy Garland, Barbara Striesand, Loretta Lynn, Billie Holliday, Bette Midler, Dottie West, Dolly Parton, Aretha Franklin, Tammy Wynette, Tina Turner, Tayna Tucker, Barbara Mandrell, Reba McEntire, Madonna, K. D. Lang, K. T. Oslin, Pearl Bailey, Brenda Lee, Dionne Warwick, Patty LaBelle, Whitney Huston, Cher and many more who have worked hard to create a place in a business that is extremely competitive and hasn't always been as kind to women as to men. These women did it their way, did it very well, and succeeded.

Women still are out-numbered by men in the music industry, but the 1990s added many new female vocalists, the two youngest, in a very long time, are the rare talents, LeAnn Rimes (Curb Records in Nashville) and Tamia (Quincy Jones in California). There seems to be a theory in the business that women buy records mainly because they are attracted to the male singer. I believe this theory is unfounded, because today's woman also buys records made by other women. Not only do they get good music from these female singers, they also observe them for fashion trends—tips on hair styles, cosmetics, fads in clothing, and health issues. There are many talented, trend-setting females with great taste in music, styles, and other women like to emulate them.

Women are proving to be assets to the business side of the music industry as well. They are excelling as managers, agents, attorneys, accountants, audio engineers, record and videos producers, publishers, broadcasters and media specialists. The opportunities are endless: Dolly owns a theme park, Barbara Mandrell has a TV series, and "Miss Reba" owns her own film production company. A woman who is highly respected in the business of writing music is Sheila Davis.

Sheila Davis is a lyricist, composer, author, and teacher. She has served as the executive vice-president of the Songwriter's Guild of America and created the critique sessions and Ask-a-Pro, a songwriter's forum which was conducted regularly in New York, Nashville and Los Angeles. She also conducted seminars on successful songwriting for songwriting associations and colleges, has written the international hit "Who Will Answer" (translated into French and Japanese). In addition, she is the author of "Successful Lyric Writing" a step-by-step work book for songwriters, "The Craft of Lyric Writing", and "Songwriters Idea Book". At the time of publication, Ms. Davis has taken time out of lecturing and giving seminars to work on yet another book for songwriters. To find out about future seminars in your area write to:

SONGCRAFT SEMINARS
441 East 20th Street
Suite 11B
New York, NY 10010
(212) 674-1143

The power of women to achieve their goals, if given the opportunity, should not be underestimated. So I say to all of you aspiring females (and male) singers: Forget the statistics and simply learn from the pioneering men and women who have gone before you.

SUMMARY OF PART IV

AFTER YOU ACHIEVE SUCCESS YOU WILL NEED TO:

- Know the people you travel with
- Purchase or rent a motor coach
- Know how to receive awards and treat fans fairly
- Women in the Business

When you have made it to the top of the music industry and reached star status, you will deserve your new position. You will have worked very hard for your "overnight" success. Be proud of your new status. If you remember to stay grounded, to treat people fairly, and to enjoy what you do, you can remain a superstar for a long time. Nobody stated it better than Vince Gill's father when he said, "...Going from bar rooms to the Grand Ole Opry doesn't mean a thing if you don't stay the same." Vince has remained the same. He sings with confidence and style. He knows who he is, where he came from, and does not mind sharing the limelight with others; he's grounded.

CONCLUSION

We have nothing to fear
but fear itself…
—Franklin D. Roosevelt

You have but one life in which to fail or succeed in your endeavors. Remember, failures are only stepping stones to success. You have to try something before you can fail at it. We all have had failures before we got it right: failed an exam, failed in a business venture, failed to get the loan, the house, car, or job we wanted. But those failures showed us where our weak and strong points were—the next time we tried, we got it right. Being afraid to try may ensure that you'll never experience the agony of defeat—but you'll never experience the thrill of success, either. There is an old saying: Nobody ever succeeded unless a whole lot of other people wanted them to. So work as hard as you can, but if you are also good at networking and are a good team player, you increase your chances of succeeding. No one can guarantee your success. The "Singer's Career Guide" has shown you the way. It has taken you from the first note sung, all the way to choosing your music city and how to start networking when you get there. It has, through proven examples of others, shown you how to stay on top once you have taken the final step. The rest is up to you. If you are a determined individual, and truly dedicated to your craft, the music business is one where anyone who is talented and understands the business can make it. Good luck and God speed!

Kathy, thank you for all the support you have given me! I will miss you!

5/28/3

ABOUT THE AUTHOR

Peggy M. Crocker resides in the beautiful Shenandoah Valley near Winchester, Virginia. During, and after, a seventeen-year career with IBM she has interviewed, written about, photographed and booked many local and regional bands, clubs and singers, as well as many of Nashville's major recording artists. For several years she has written articles and created ads for the *Country Plus* magazine, a metropolitan Washington entertainment publication that specializes in country music. (One of the articles, from an interview with Patsy Cline's sister, Sylvia, was quoted three times in a published book about the early life of Patsy Cline.)

In order to research for this book, Ms. Crocker has owned and operated a modern nightclub, promoted and staged concerts, worked in an agent/management capacity, worked with an agency in Nashville at the Nashville buyers/sellers convention, and spent the past twenty years learning the craft of the music industry. She spent three years working at the Wayside Theatre, an equity actors live stage performing theatre in Middletown, Virginia, learning the craft of sound, lights, stage production techniques, and stage management. She has studied and researched various facets of the entertainment industry and has a business degree from the Shenandoah University and Conservatory of Music in Winchester, Virginia. She earned a graduate degree in Business from Strayer University, in Manassas, Virginia.

Crocker is a member of the Independent Writer's Group of Washington, D.C., a member of the Shenandoah Writer's Group of the Shenandoah Valley, and is a member of the Country Music Association in Nashville.

Printed in the United States
1038400001B/229-246